ALMOST HUMAN

**ALFRED
FIDJESTØL**

ALMOST
HUMAN

The Story of Julius,
the Chimpanzee Caught
between Two Worlds

TRANSLATED BY
BECKY L. CROOK

GREYSTONE BOOKS
Vancouver/Berkeley

Greystone Books Ltd.
greystonebooks.com

Cataloguing data available from Library and Archives Canada
ISBN 978-1-77164-385-6 (cloth)
ISBN 978-1-77164-386-3 (epub)

Editing by Heather Wood
Proofreading by Alison Strobel
Indexing by Stephen Ullstrom
Jacket and text design by Nayeli Jimenez
Jacket photographs by Arild Jakobsen

Printed   by Friesens

Greys   quamish
an   cated.

rts,

the Br   Columbia
th   ment

LONDON BOROUGH OF WANDSWORTH	
9030 00007 0293 3	
Askews & Holts	30-Jan-2020
636.988509	£18.99
	WW19016164

Canada Council   Conseil des arts
for the Arts   du Canada

CONTENTS

INTRODUCTION

KNOW IT IS a strange thing to read a biography about a
chimpanzee. For people in other countries, it must feel even
stranger to read about one specific Norwegian chimpanzee
who, though he may enjoy celebrity status in Norway, is a
completely unknown to the rest of the world. Nevertheless,
there is something about this chimpanzee's life that fascinates
and amazes across borders.

Julius the chimpanzee was born in a zoo in the small city of
Kristiansand in southern Norway on the day after Christmas
in 1979. His mother rejected him, his keepers found him in a
pool of blood with an index finger bitten off, and he had to be
rescued from the community of chimpanzees and taken to
live among humans. Although he was eventually reintegrated
with the other chimps, for a long time his life followed the
path of a classic tragedy. His misfortune at a young age distinguished him from the others, and he was a misfit among his
peers and bullied by the other chimpanzees. As he grew larger,
it was no longer possible for him to seek contact and comfort
from humans. He became homeless in both worlds. Because

he managed to break out of the chimpanzee enclosure on multiple occasions and attacked zoo employees, he had to be kept in isolation in an escape-proof cage. It was only in 2005 that a fortunate turn of events allowed Julius to be reintegrated into the zoo's chimpanzee community as its leader.

It sometimes happens that certain, select animals achieve international celebrity status, such as the chimpanzee Cheeta from the Tarzan films, the gorilla Koko who communicated via sign language, or the German polar bear, Knut. Julius, the Norwegian chimpanzee, is unique among these celebrity animals because his forty-year life span has been so well documented and sourced that it was possible to hold to standard biographical methods, following the same documentation and evidence requirements as those of a human biography. It was possible to write about his life with only one, tiny deviation from the usual modern biography: namely that the subject of this biography is not, nor ever has been, human. Only almost.

There is something about the nature of a chimpanzee that makes it a particularly suitable biographical subject. A chimpanzee is so much more than an animal merely reacting on instinct to stimuli and physiological needs. Individual chimps are able to make decisions and take actions that impact the entire course of their lives. Their memories are impressively intact, and they are influenced and shaped by events that occurred earlier in their lives. Julius has an extremely close emotional bond to the humans with whom he lived forty years ago. They still love each other, even if it is dangerous for them to be in the same room together. This is why writing a chimpanzee biography, with the same sincerity and according to the same rigorous factual standards essential to a modern human biography, is also a political act of sorts. Humans are not the only animals with unique life spans that are influenced by our choices and experiences. Nor are we singular in the universe in being suitable biographical subjects. The story of Julius is also a story about the changing perception of animals. When the first big city zoos were established in the 1800s, they existed primarily to showcase humankind's dominion over nature. Animals were degraded and put into small cages so people could saunter around them in safety and observe the beasts in triumph. When Julius was born, zookeepers still knew relatively little about the advanced social and intellectual needs of chimpanzees. However, over the course of his life, both his zoo and zoos around the world have undergone a valuable learning process. Today, chimpanzees in Julius's community are respected and handled as unique individuals with social and emotional needs. Modern zoos no longer exist to humiliate animals but act rather to protect and preserve species whose extinction is being threatened in the wild.

This biography about Julius is an independent and unvarnished version of how one particular chimpanzee's life unfolded. I have never worked for nor had any connection to the zoo in Kristiansand. Personally, my relationship to Julius is no more intimate than is the case for most Norwegians of my generation. And yet, no other animal in the world is more closely linked to me than he is. Julius and I share 98.6 percent of our genetic material. From an evolutionary perspective, it was only a short time ago that our species parted ways, or more specifically, it has been only a mere six million years since our common "great-grandmother" was alive. My hemoglobin molecule, the protein that transports oxygen and gives blood its red color, is in all of its 287 entities completely identical to Julius's. Even several details of our individual life stories resemble one another's. Both of us were born into similar conditions in the small social democratic nation of Norway in the 1970s. Both of us grew up as members of families with two older siblings and parents. We are able to eat roughly the same diet, are both more or less the same size as adults, and we have both become the fathers of three children.

This resemblance—in spite of the great divide between our species—fanned my curiosity about Julius as a biographical subject. I was not only curious about the course of his life, but also about what I might be able to discover about his world. I wanted to employ international research about both wild and captive chimpanzees to uncover as much as possible about what is going on behind those dark, mysterious eyes of his.

Several times while working on this book, I sat in the Kristiansand Zoo, staring into Julius's eyes. It is a strange feeling—different from staring into the eyes of other animals. There is something recognizable if you peer deep into the chimpanzee gaze. And there is also something totally foreign. I can't quite put my finger on what it is. This book is an attempt to find out.

Chapter 1

NATURE AND NURTURE

*"Whatever happens happens. We will deal
with it later. We can't just stand here watching
the baby die before our eyes."* [1]

WILLIAM (BILLY) GLAD

THE HEART IS a mysterious muscle. It starts to beat in one
moment and then, at some other moment, the beating
stops. No one knows the precise reason why a fetus's heart
suddenly starts to beat while in its mother's womb. No one
knows why the first electrical impulse in the heart chamber
sends a message to the heart commanding it to contract and,
for the first time, pump blood out through tiny, narrow arter-
ies. For a chimpanzee fetus, which gestates in the womb for
eight months, the first heartbeat occurs around six weeks. So,
the heart of the chimpanzee who is the subject of this book
must have felt its very first heartbeat sometime in May of 1979,
possibly even on the 17th of May, the Norwegian national holiday, when King Olav stood on the palace balcony in Oslo

during a mild spring drizzle and waved down at the annual children's parade.[2] And even today, forty years later, this same heart muscle continues to beat strongly and rhythmically, day in and day out, within the chest of a now fully grown chimpanzee, who resides in a zoo in Kristiansand, in southern Norway.

No one can say exactly when that first heartbeat took place. Observant zookeepers may have taken note that a female chimp named Sanne had failed to ovulate that month. It is simple enough to spot ovulation in female chimpanzees through their pink, swollen genitalia. However, it was only after her cycle failed to appear month after month during the summer of 1979 that Sanne's pregnancy became clear to the zookeepers. As the birth approached, they did not take any special measures for medical assistance from veterinarians or keepers. The birth of a chimpanzee is less complicated than a human's. Stillbirth is extremely rare. In the wild, chimpanzees climb a tree when they sense the birth approaching and the laboring mother conducts the entire affair alone. At some point or other during the night between Christmas and December 26, 1979, Sanne gave birth to a small chimpanzee weighing 3.3 pounds. She must have pushed the tiny fetus out unobserved, cleaned it off with nearby pieces of straw and settled down with the newborn, which was still attached by the umbilical cord.

In the morning, keeper Åse Gunn Mosvold arrived on duty. It was a quiet day at the zoo. No visitors had arrived yet and there were few staff members at work. As usual, she first went to the kitchen to put the water on for porridge before checking on the chimps. The chimpanzees were housed inside of the so-called Tropical House for the winter. This enclosure provided them with space to move about in a common area where visitors could view them. There were walls of moss green clay blocks, a steep rock formation surrounded by water, and upright timber beams and green climbing ropes criss-crossing here and there. Behind the scenes, a private sleeping partition was located near the zookeeper kitchen. The chimps were still lounging on the floor inside their sleeping quarters that morning. The group was peaceful and quiet. It was an idyllic scene. Suddenly, Mosvold noticed the reclining Sanne clutching a small chimpanzee baby in her arms, and the umbilical cord that had come loose in the straw. The whole chimp community seemed to quietly accept the new arrival. They paid him scant attention and continued their languid snoozing. "Sanne gave birth in the night! Everything appears to be in excellent condition now, 12:30 p.m. Sanne is lying on the rocks, the baby is on her stomach, high up on her stomach, which is a good sign," Mosvold noted in the daily observation report for December 26, 1979.[3] The tiny chimp had found its way to its mother's breast and began to feed for the first time.

In its earliest days, the infant chimp didn't need to do anything other than hold onto its mother. Chimpanzee babies are entirely dependent on their mothers for several years. Humans share this trait with them. A newborn chimp's fingers or toes will curl around a finger held up against its palms or feet. This is an evolutionary adaptation. Humans share these reflexes with them. We are built to cling to our mothers.

A NEW COMMUNITY

Åse Gunn Mosvold was given the honor of naming the chimp. Seeing as the animal was born during the Christmas season (*jul* in Norwegian), and she believed it to be a girl, Mosvold dubbed it Juliane. Later, when the chimp was discovered to be male, the name was adapted to Julius.[4]

The chimpanzee community into which Julius was born was small and relatively new. The Kristiansand Zoo had only recently acquired chimpanzees. Founded in 1965, the zoo was a somewhat haphazard project located in a no man's land along the E18 highway, almost six miles from the nearest house. Goats, swans, ponies, baboons and brown bears were the largest attractions in the first years. However, Edvard Moseid, the eccentric and animal-loving gardener who became the park's director in 1967, had greater ambitions. Moseid looked like a hippy, sporting long hair, a mustache and an ever-present cigarette protruding from his lips. But he possessed an otherworldly knack for animals and, as would prove later, a uniquely commercial flair. In 1969, he imported twenty camels from the Moscow Zoo. His plan was to initiate camel breeding and export them to the United States of America. Due to the Cold War, the United States refused to import directly from the Soviet Union. Importing second-generation camels via Kristiansand, however, was completely acceptable. And so for nearly a decade, the exporting of camels became a primary source of income for the zoo. Year after year, the park was expanded and upgraded, new varieties of animals were added and, in 1976, Moseid was finally able to bring in the first generation of the particular species that all self-respecting, ambitious zookeepers dream of—chimpanzees. On January 13, 1976, the Royal Norwegian Ministry of Agriculture and Food issued a decision allowing the Kristiansand Zoo to import four chimpanzees from the Jylland Mini Zoo in Herning, Denmark.[5] Eight days later, on January 21, 1976, Director Moseid was on board the Danish ferry from Hirtshals to Kristiansand with four chimpanzee passengers in his car. Among them was Sanne, who would later become Julius's mother. Moseid transported the chimps in individual dog crates, which he then lugged one by one from the car up to his berth. It was a night crossing and there were strong winds and towering waves. All four chimpanzees got seasick and vomited throughout the entire duration of the trip. After finally arriving at the zoo, they were held in quarantine inside the old camel stalls as required by the Ministry of Agriculture. One of the chimps, which turned out to be sick and unsuitable for public presentation, was shipped back. Another had to be put down a year later on suspicion of tuberculosis. The only two remaining chimps were Sanne and a small male named Polle. For this reason, the zoo requested permission from the Ministry of Agriculture in March of 1977 to import two additional adult chimpanzees from the Borås Zoo in Sweden, a male and a female, named Dennis and Lotta. They were ten and nine years old, respectively, when they arrived by car to Kristiansand. With the arrival of Dennis, the community had acquired a potential alpha chimp. Later that same year, two younger female chimpanzees, Skinny and Bølla, were brought in from the Faavang Zoo in Denmark. The Danish zookeeper believed them to be under two years of age, though he couldn't be certain. Both had been captured in the wild.[6]

Skinny and Polle both died before Julius was born. A few months earlier, Lotta had given birth to a small male chimpanzee named Billy. Dennis, the alpha male, had become a proud father of two in a very short time. In the first few days, the relationship between Julius and Sanne appeared promising. Sanne was a caring mother. She and Dennis would sit for long periods watching the baby, cuddling and presenting him to one another.[7] It was the middle of winter, and they were indoors with little to do. They would lie together and groom each other's fur, an important activity for chimpanzees, which involves picking out and killing your partner's lice.

Chimpanzees in captivity have quite a lot of time for this sort of activity. In the wild, chimpanzees spend half of their waking hours either eating or going in search of food.[8] They wander about in groups, hunting for food, stopping frequently to overnight in new places, often in the location of their last meal. In these spots, they build small nests high up in the trees where they spend the night. In captivity, there is nowhere to go. The chimps' every meal is served by humans, though during this early period, Julius was not supposed to receive any other kind of food than his mother's milk.

The family TV series *Norge Rundt* (Around Norway), which aired on the NRK station, presented a special feature on the two first chimpanzees born into captivity in Norway. The zoo's doctor, William (Billy) Glad, after whom the chimp Billy was named, informed viewers that so far Sanne had been a good mother. Sanne had studied Lotta's childcare regimen during her pregnancy and appeared well prepared, Billy Glad told the Norwegian people during the episode.[9]

A few weeks later, however, toward the end of January 1980, the keepers began to notice the first signs indicating that Sanne's behavior toward little Julius wasn't so rosy after all. Her attitude changed abruptly. She began to put Julius down while she went off to do other things. He was left lying alone for extended periods. It didn't seem to bother Sanne that he would lie there whimpering. In the jungle, a lone chimp baby would become a quick meal for predators, or even other chimpanzees, if left alone in this way. The father and alpha male, Dennis, was visibly irritated. Every now and then he would go over and nudge the baby, perhaps to send a kind of signal to Sanne to return and resume caring for him.

Sometimes, the younger female chimp, Bølla, would step in as a type of substitute mother, but she did not have breast milk to offer, and the keepers once had to intervene and sedate her in order to remove Julius from her and return him to Sanne—who would then once more act irresponsibly. Sanne's behavioral shift was odd, resembling postpartum depression. Her keepers noted that she often left Julius to fend for himself for as long as 45 minutes at a time.[10]

YOUNG MOTHER

Sanne was a young mother, only eight years old. It is not unusual for first-time chimpanzee mothers to be somewhat indifferent to their young. While cats and birds automatically and instinctively know how to care for their offspring, chimpanzees—and humans—must learn these skills from others. It is therefore common for a chimpanzee's first pregnancy to fail, whether due to miscarriage or stillbirth or the mother's inability to care for her young. In fact, there is an evolutionary logic to the development in some species of a mechanism in which young mothers do not needlessly waste their time and resources on childrearing until they are socially mature enough to manage the task. It is common in chimpanzee colonies for young mothers to learn about motherhood from the older, more experienced females.[11] Often, a chimpanzee mother may allow a young, childless female to try out the role of keeper for her chimpanzee newborn. The mother remains nearby, assuring herself that the young female chimpanzee in training is not taking undue risks, that she is handling the baby gently, that she is not climbing too high with him and that she does leave him lying on his own. Only after such a trial period are the younger female chimps allowed to act as babysitters. Lotta had most likely picked these skills up from other mothers at the Swedish zoo and was thus able to care for Billy, while Sanne had never seen any such behavior modeled at her zoo in Denmark. Although Sanne had been able to observe Lotta's mothering for a few months, she had apparently not gleaned enough during this short period to give Julius the proper care he needed.

To complicate matters, Sanne was an unpredictable chimpanzee. Her keepers had been curious about how she would handle her role as a mother. Their routines in those days involved considerable risks, as keepers regularly entered the chimpanzee enclosures and came into close physical contact with the chimps. It usually went well enough. The keepers learned to read each individual chimpanzee and decide when it might be safe or unsafe to be in their presence. Dennis was a wise and caring chimp who was easy to figure out. Sanne, on the other hand, was unreliable and her mood could change from one second to the next. She was temperamental and hot-blooded.[12]

Now that Sanne had a baby it was no longer possible to enter the enclosure with her. It was hard enough trying to get her to change her behavior. The keepers felt helpless to do anything other than stand by, watching Julius from the outside. They tried to isolate Sanne and Julius from the rest of the group in order to encourage better emotional bonding between mother and baby, but even then she would frequently set him aside and continue to ignore him. Julius became dehydrated and overly cold from lying on the cement floor for long stretches of time and could easily have become seriously ill. On February 12, 1980, the situation took a dramatic turn. At some point or another over the course of the afternoon, unobserved, one of the other chimpanzees bit Julius's finger so hard that his fingertip was hanging loose. None of the keepers knew which chimp was the culprit and some of them believed it must have been Sanne, while others thought it clearly was Dennis's doing. It may also have been Lotta or Bølla. Only Billy was small enough to be considered innocent in the ordeal. One theory was that Dennis bit Julius in order to evoke a motherly reaction from Sanne or one of the other female chimpanzees.

The wound was discovered around 7:00 p.m. Julius was lying in a pool of blood, howling from the pain. One of the keepers quickly called Billy Glad and director Edvard Moseid, who both arrived as quickly as possible. They were onsite by 7:30 p.m. Julius was on his back, screaming. Edvard signaled that he was going to enter the pen to help Julius, but Sanne responded with a clear gesture indicating that he was not allowed. Instead, she scooped Julius up but held him carelessly and roughly at an arm's distance, away from her own body. After a short while she put him back down again, this time on his stomach in the hay. Julius appeared starved; he grew silent and seemed nearly dead. Sanne was more concerned with the three humans than with her baby's well-being. Julius was going to die if Edvard and Billy did not intervene. They felt they had no choice. They had to try to save him. "Whatever happens, happens. We will deal with it later. We can't just stand here watching the baby die before our eyes," Billy noted in his journal.[13]

Sanne flew into a rage as they came close; she did not want to let them into the enclosure. Her maternal instinct was still functioning in this single aspect. Although she ignored Julius, she now acted to protect him from intruders. Edvard tried pulling Julius out with a plastic rake, but Sanne's brutal reaction stopped him. Nor could they persuade Sanne to go into a separate pen so they enter and retrieve Julius. They tried tempting her with grapes and bananas, even with soda, but Sanne wouldn't budge. Time was running out. They had to get ahold of the chimpanzee baby. Thinking they might already be too late, they decided to fetch a hose. Billy aimed the powerful jet of water straight at Sanne, pressing her toward the back wall as Edvard opened the feeding hatch, leaned in with the rake and scooped Julius toward the fence where it was possible to coax the tiny creature under it and out of the enclosure.[14]

It was 8:15 p.m. when Billy finally held Julius in his arms. Julius smelled bad and was dirty, his fingertip dangled loosely with a bone sticking out. Billy wrapped him inside of a blue wool sweater and a military jacket while Edvard sprinted down to the office to call Billy's wife, Reidun. He informed her that a party was on its way to their house in Bliksheia with a small baby chimpanzee.

"That's fine," she replied.[15] They administered a few teaspoons of sugary water to Julius before carrying him down to the parking lot where they stowed him in the front seat of Billy's car and drove home to the Glad family. Here Julius would remain for a few days until his health improved and his finger healed. No one knew what would happen after that. There was no plan. From here on out, it was all improvisation.

Chapter 2

HAPPY DAYS

"If we look straight and deep into a chimpanzee's eyes,
an intelligent, self-assured personality looks back at us.
If they are animals, what must we be?" [16]

FRANS DE WAAL

ILLY AND REIDUN Glad's two sons, twelve-year-old Carl Christian and ten-year-old Øystein, were still awake when their father and Edvard Moseid parked the car outside the house and stormed into the living room with a baby chimpanzee in their arms. Outside it was cold and dark, snowy and blustery. Julius stared at the two boys with wide, terrified eyes. Edvard placed Julius on the kitchen table and Billy snipped off the torn tendon protruding from his fingertip, rinsed and bandaged the wound, affixed the damaged finger to two other fingers and gave Julius pain killers. Then he cleaned the chimp's entire body with a cloth and dressed him in a wool shirt. Reidun went down to the cellar and found an old nursing bottle from her own sons' infant days. She filled it with warm milk, thinned out somewhat with water and gave Julius a few small sips at a time. She held him on her lap as she fed him and Julius began to relax.[17] Later that evening he was fed again, this time with a bit of penicillin mixed in. They put him in a banana box in the bathroom, the warmest room in the house. He made a few small whimpering sounds and fell asleep. Only hours before, he had been a member of a community of captive chimpanzees, and while neglected by his mother, he was nonetheless surrounded by his own kind. Now here he was, asleep in a human's bathroom.

Edvard had recently moved to a new house in Vennesla, a community neighboring Kristiansand, and he had two small daughters aged two and four. They therefore agreed that Julius would live with the Glads for the first weeks. The Glad children were older; Reidun was a stay-at-home mom with a nursing background. Billy was a medical doctor—not a veterinarian—but had nonetheless assumed responsibility for the medical needs of the zoo's chimpanzees, considering it an intriguing challenge.

The Glads decided not to let Julius sleep alone for the first night in his new quarters. Reidun dragged a mattress into the bathroom and put it on the floor beside him. Her night was sleepless and full of wonder; Julius slept surprisingly deeply. He woke up hungry once and she gave him a new bottle of milk. After that, he burped in satisfaction before falling back asleep. In his sleep, he sucked on his left thumb.[18]

When he woke up in the morning, Julius appeared to have a high temperature. At first, Billy worried that the chimp had a fever but he soon realized that the floor heaters in the bathroom had been too turned up too high. Julius was healthy and content. He drank more, urinated as he should and appeared altogether safe. He quickly formed a bond with Reidun as his mother and preferred to snuggle in her arms at all times, while she patted and stroked his fur.

Chimpanzee and other primate infants have an intense yearning for bodily contact. To show this, the American psychologist, Harry Harlow, conducted a heart-wrenching experiment in the 1950s. Harlow removed rhesus monkeys from their mothers directly following childbirth and instead placed them with artificial surrogates devised from steel wire and made to resemble their mothers. He put two different "surrogate mothers" into each cage: one mother was nothing but a steel wire contraption holding a bottle of formula milk, not reminiscent of any kind of animal, and the other mother did not have any formula to offer but was covered with soft fabric that looked like a stuffed monkey. The theory was that the monkey babies would prioritize the "mother" with the milk, proving that they only required nourishment and not connection. The results, however, showed that all of the babies prioritized the soft "mother," the one who had nothing more to offer than her own plush. Harlow tried to correct the findings by fastening an electric bulb to the doll with the formula so that she would be at least as warm as the soft alternative, but the babies continued to favor the downy mother. They would drink what they needed from the hard "mother" and then return to spend most of their time with the soft doll.[19] In other words, they craved emotional bonds as much as milk. They needed love as much as they needed food. Now Reidun had become a surrogate mother for Julius. The same human source offered him both milk and touch. He could recline comfortably in her lap and receive all of the physical contact, care and attention that had been absent for him amongst the chimpanzees.

"IT IS AN ANIMAL"

The Glad family quickly grew accustomed to the new situation. Billy was impressed by the ability of his sons to adapt to the new reality. Firstly, they managed to keep the fact that they were housing a baby chimpanzee at home under wraps, even though their hearts were nearly bursting at the seams with the world's biggest secret. Secondly, they accepted the unknown. Their parents told them repeatedly that Julius was only an animal, that he might have to be put down eventually and that, in any case, he would certainly not remain in their home long-term, like a baby brother.[20] And thirdly, they were good with Julius. The two boys passed time sprawled out on the floor with Julius, trying to communicate with him as their father had instructed them to do. They would make soft "oo-oo" noises and receive squeaking communication attempts back from Julius. Just as human children, young chimpanzees play at taking turns when learning to communicate. The baby chimps and the adult chimpanzees alternate at making noises and listening. In this way, the young are able to learn the basic methods for communicating.[21] The Glad brothers were simultaneously playing with Julius and imparting him with vital communication skills.

Reidun bought human breast milk formula so that Julius would no longer have to drink watered-down milk. And they decided to dress him in disposable diapers so they wouldn't have to keep cleaning up his messes. In general, they wanted to raise him as much as possible like a chimpanzee but on this one important point they simply had to compromise. Julius slept often and peacefully in his cardboard box, preferring to lie on his stomach with his legs pulled up beneath his body and his head turned to the side. After a few days, he became more animated, and it was easier to interact with him. He began to try out more noises and every now and then stretched his toothless mouth wide open. He was able to sit partway up in the box on his own and to follow sounds with his eyes. Chimpanzees' sensory apparatus is much like our own. They have a similar sensitivity to light and the ability to distinguish between different wavelengths. Chimps have color vision, though humans appear to be more sensitive to the yellow-red end of the spectrum. In general, chimpanzees have a better sense of sound than we do and are better equipped to hear high frequency noises. They also possess a much better sense of smell.[22] Julius watched and listened to the humans around him and could sense strong, strange and unfamiliar smells: the smell of humans, of clothing and furniture, milk and human food.

Though his general condition improved, beneath the bandages his finger smelled of infection. Billy changed the bandages every day, rinsed the wound and administered antibiotics through shots in Julius's leg, but still his finger refused to heal. For this reason, on February 21, after nine days at the Glad family house, chief physician Helge Svendsen from the West Agder Central Hospital arrived with his operating equipment. With nurse Reidun Glad assisting, Julius was given 2 milligrams of Rohypnol blended in milk and a local anesthetic before his fingertip was amputated on the Glad family kitchen counter.[23]

Though the surgery was a success, Julius remained completely limp after the operation. It was difficult to rouse and feed him. Four days passed before he became his usual self again. He began to eat and make noises, responding happily if provoked by someone. He now weighed 7 pounds, had built up muscles on his back and body and was able to sit up in his box by holding onto the sides. Over the next few days, his development picked up speed. If the Glad family held his hands, he was able to pull himself to stand.

Naturally, the entire Glad family grew dangerously fond of Julius. For Reidun, who was at home with him during the day while the others were at work or school, the situation reminded her a little too much of the earlier period of her life when she was the mother of two small children. It was the way she held Julius and fed him his bottle, or changed his diapers, as well as the way in which he lovingly responded to her care. The last time she had carried out such tasks, her activities had been accompanied by an intense motherly love. Now she was required to go through the same motions while all the time reminding herself that Julius was only an animal in her arms, and not a human being. Billy struggled as well: "It is an animal. His time with us is limited," he lectured himself.[24]

On February 28, zoo director Edvard Moseid arrived to take Julius to his own house in Vennesla. They wanted to see how Julius would react to a change of environment, and they also wanted to prevent him from forming strong attachments to a single family. But as Edvard carried Julius out to his car, the chimp began to howl. He howled all the way from

Kristiansand to Vennesla. He was then apathetic for the entire first day in Vennesla, but when he began to understand that he was just as safe among these new humans as he had been with the Glad family, he started adapting to his new surroundings.

The Moseid family was definitely animal friendly. Before moving to Vennesla, Edvard and Marit Moseid and their two young daughters, Ane and Siv, had lived on a small farm in Lillesand where they had had a standing agreement with the agricultural authorities that their farm could function as a quarantine zone for animals imported to the zoo. The family thus had a history of caring for snakes, crocodiles, hippos and lizards and even a fully grown sea lion.[25] Julius, however, was something else entirely. He was like a tiny infant and the Moseid girls were warned that they had to be very careful when handling him. They whispered when they were around Julius and gently petted his coat. Just like a human child, he loved to be rubbed on the chest or tickled under his arms and neck. A baby chimpanzee reacts to tickling in almost the same manner that a human child does—he laughs with an open mouth when he is tickled, displaying the same ambivalence as a human child, appearing as though it likes and doesn't like tickling at the same time, and can even start laughing if one merely points at a sensitive area.[26]

Julius began to bond with Marit as a second surrogate mother. When she returned Julius to Reidun after one week in Vennesla, Julius again became confused and apathetic. But after just one day back in the Glad home, he returned to his usual behavior. Billy had doubted whether Julius would manage the shift but became more optimistic after seeing how the chimpanzee was able to flip-flop between the two families.

Eventually, Moseid and Glad hoped to incorporate the zoo-keeper Grete Svendsen into the rotation, since she was the person who would take over responsibility for Julius's daily supervision when—or if—he was returned to his chimpanzee community at the zoo.

SKINNY'S "MURDER"

The big question on everyone's mind was how to proceed with integrating Julius back into the chimpanzee community. Edvard and Billy knew they needed help. They had seen the fallout resulting from a previous miscommunication between a new chimp and the community. A small chimpanzee, Skinny, who had been imported from Denmark together with Bølla in 1977, was murdered by the group in Kristiansand. Skinny and Bølla had been the only two chimpanzees in the Danish zoo. They had thus never learned how to interact and communicate with other chimpanzees.[27] On top of that, Skinny had been captured in the wild and must have lived with humans for a period before arriving in a zoo. She had never learned the proper chimpanzee language and behaviors and instead used simple gestures and movements that she had picked up from humans, gestures that her fellow chimpanzees in Kristiansand interpreted as aggressive challenges. Lotta was particularly angry at Skinny and once bit off two of her toes. The toes were not completely severed but remained hanging from her foot. The veterinarian Gudbrand Hval and Billy Glad decided to operate. They brought Skinny home to one of the keeper's apartments and put her under anesthesia by placing a cloth with trichloroethylene over her mouth. Using pliers from the zoo's janitor, which they boiled in water on the stove and disinfected with alcohol, Billy Glad was able to perform a successful operation. In order to protect Skinny in the future, the keepers created a small shutter door leading away from the common chimp enclosure into an individual pen where Skinny could retreat to safety whenever she felt threatened. However, a keeper had forgotten to leave the shutter door open one evening, and when the staff arrived back at work the next day, June 30, 1978, Skinny was dead. "Presumed killed in the group," stated the note in the formal annual animal review issued to the Ministry of Agriculture.[28] In fact, Dennis had hoisted her up and slammed her against the cement wall. The autopsy report revealed a fracture on her skull and profuse bleeding in Skinny's brain.

Being killed was one possible fate that might await Julius upon his return to the group. One step out of line, and he wouldn't stand a chance. Glad and Moseid pored over international studies on chimpanzees and contacted other European zoos requesting assistance. In 1980, they went on a whirlwind research trip to Switzerland and the Netherlands to speak with some of the leading experts in the field. They visited zoos in Zurich and Basel in Switzerland and the Royal Burgers' Zoo in Arnhem in the Netherlands. Basel housed around twenty to thirty chimpanzees, and the park had recently completed a successful reintegration of what Glad and Moseid later learned to call a "hand-raised" chimpanzee. The Arnhem zoo in the Netherlands had forty chimpanzees and a wealth of experience reintegrating chimpanzees that had formerly been outcasts. This zoo also boasted practical and scientific facilities that boggled the minds of the two Norwegians. There were examination rooms, operating rooms, individual sick rooms, quarantine rooms, a lab and two full-time biologists. In addition, the thirty-one-year-old, soon to be world-renowned zoologist, Frans de Waal, was at the park every day.

At the time of their visit, de Waal was in the middle of writing what would later be one of the most widely-read chimpanzee books of all time, *Chimpanzee Politics*.[29] Frans de Waal studied the social structures within the Arnhem community, sitting on a stool for thousands of hours while observing and taking notes. Inspired by the political theories of Italian Renaissance philosopher, Niccolò Machiavelli, de Waal analyzed the intricate power play between the chimpanzees, interactions that he dubbed "chimpanzee politics." One example from the book portrays a fight, which occurred in the summer of 1976. It began when a chimpanzee named Luit challenged the alpha male, Yeroen, by taking sexual matters into his own hands and openly mating with one of the female chimps without permission from Yeroen. After this, Luit began challenging the alpha male using a variety of subtle tactics aimed more at winning over Yeroen's previous allies to his own side than in seeking a physical confrontation. Luit suddenly began to spend much more time together with the females who had previously supported Yeroen. He cuddled with them, groomed their fur and began playing with their young—not unlike a U.S. presidential candidate kissing babies on the campaign trail. Luit taught himself to climb one of the enclosure's more difficult trees where he was able to pick fresh leaves that were popular among the chimpanzees. He would then distribute these coveted leaves magnanimously amongst his "supporters." The decisive strategic turning point came when Luit won approval from the most important male chimp, Nikkie, a sort of second in command or vice president. On the seventy-second day after Luit had initiated his challenge, Yeroen admitted defeat. He greeted Luit submissively for the first time, thereby installing Luit as the new leader of the chimpanzee community.[30]

Moseid and Glad listened attentively to all that de Waal and the Arnhem zookeepers told them, particularly their knowledge about the reintegration of outcast chimpanzee babies. A deaf female chimp in Arnhem was constantly giving birth to new chimpanzees, but she was unable to care for them as a result of her handicap. Infant chimpanzees communicate verbally from birth, making small, nearly silent whimpering noises. The deaf chimpanzee was unable to react to these signals and prompts from her young.[31] Still, the zoo administrators had chosen not to give her a contraceptive implant and instead allowed her to become pregnant multiple times. Each time she gave birth, however, the infant would die within weeks. Eventually, they had decided to remove the babies right after birth and attempt various strategies for introducing them back into the community. In 1979, the same year of Julius's birth, they had succeeded in teaching another female chimp how to take over caring for a baby and feeding it milk from a bottle. The surrogate mother had first received training in her cage on how to handle the nursing bottle and was rewarded whenever she did it correctly. When the baby was two weeks old, she assumed responsibility for its well-being and proved to be a caring foster mother. She fed the young chimpanzee calmly and lovingly with the bottle and even acted in clever ways they had not taught her, such as lifting the baby upright, allowing him to gulp if he had trouble drinking. After a week with the nursing bottle, the adoptive mother began producing her own supply of breast milk and could soon offer the baby half of its required nourishment. On another occasion, when they were forced to raise another newborn chimp among humans for a few weeks, they reintegrated the infant by employing a female chimp whose baby had died shortly after birth. They rushed to the zoo with the human-raised chimp baby and placed it in the arms of the mourning mother, who immediately began to care for the baby.[32]

Kristiansand Zoo, unfortunately, did not have any of these options for Julius. None of the adult chimpanzees had been trained to feed with a bottle and there were no new mothers who had recently lost their young. As it was, Lotta had her hands full with her own son, Billy. Julius's mother Sanne apparently did not want anything to do with him and Bølla was too young. Julius would therefore have to remain among humans until he was safe and strong enough to be able to return and care for himself. Safety thus became the highest priority for the coming phase. In the spring of 1980, his keepers would try to provide for his welfare through three different groups: the Glad group, the Moseid group and what might be called the Zoo group, with keeper Grete Svendsen as the key group member. The idea was to get Julius used to spending time with Svendsen at the zoo and eventually moving him into his own cage from where he would be able to watch and hear the other chimpanzees. It was essential that he learn proper chimpanzee behavior firsthand. It was also important for Julius to establish regular eye and sound contact with the other chimpanzee community members. His keepers would have to allow for a sufficient period of time to pass between establishing first visual contact and the moment when Julius would finally be allowed to come into physical contact with another chimpanzee. How long this waiting period might be was anyone's guess. Glad and Moseid were offered mixed advice on the topic: In Basel, someone recommended they begin establishing first contact when Julius was only six months old. In Arnhem, the advice was to wait until Julius was two years old.[33]

A VISIT TO THE ZOO

When Billy Glad first returned home from Arnhem, Julius treated him like a stranger. Billy had only been absent for a few days, but Julius now acted afraid of him and clung to Reidun. After a while, Julius again recognized Billy as familiar and became as confident and trusting as he had been before. Julius was developing well both psychologically and physically. At only two months old, he had made his first attempts to crawl and had taught himself to balance on all four legs. By three months of age, he was able to crawl around on the slippery bathroom tiles. And he had even started to walk around on his hind legs. He grew teeth and tried them out on books and furniture, door frames and cupboard doors, acquiring an especially fond taste for the Glad family's charity receipts from the Norwegian Rescue Mission.[34] In March he began eating solid foods and was offered baby food, which he hated with a passion. It took heaps of patience and spilled mush before Julius finally got used to the human fare.

Julius began to live more and more frequently with the Moseid family, and Edvard Moseid often brought Julius to the zoo so that he could spend time alone with Grete Svendsen. She fed him milk from a bottle without any resistance. Julius seemed to be accepting of everything that they wanted him to accept. Their devised system of the three "family groups" appeared to have worked. The only problem was that Julius had become more and more dependent on human attention. He no longer wanted to be put down after his feeding but insisted on playing and being entertained. This exhausted his human keepers, particularly Edvard, who had more than enough to do already as the father of two small children and a zoo director. The zoo now had more than 200,000 visitors per year and hosted a wide variety of species, from brown bears to kangaroos. It had turned into a complex logistical operation involving the production and the importation of various types of feed, organizing and caring for all of the different species, ensuring safety procedures for the employees and humane conditions for the animals, marketing and planning for the future. Moseid's mind was constantly brimming with new ideas. He dreamed of establishing a zoo hotel complete with a swim hall and solarium.[35] On top of everything else, he was mourning the loss of a cousin in the tragic oil platform accident of March 27, 1980, when the *Alexander Kielland* capsized in the Ekofisk oil field in the North Sea, killing 123 people on board. In the midst of all of this, he was now responsible for the care of a baby chimpanzee at home.

Reidun also began to feel the strain of looking after Julius. During the weeks when Julius lived with the Glads, she couldn't let him out of her sight. If she tried to accomplish any other task while he was awake, he would howl loudly for her attention. "It's high time he moved out," Billy noted on April 14, 1980.[36]

At the end of April, the Glad and Moseid families, plus Grete Svendsen, met at the zoo to introduce Julius to the chimpanzee community for the first time. Julius was now four months old and had been separated from the other chimps for two and a half months. A cot had been set up for Julius near the window of the private sleeping quarters, and the other chimpanzees would be able to see Julius through a window. It was the first small step on a long road back. They put Julius down on his cot, opened the flap between the common enclosure and the sleeping quarters and waited. His mother Sanne was the first to come in. Julius whimpered and Sanne made a trumpet shape with her mouth and a sound they had not heard before. But she was otherwise uninterested, though she did not appear upset. The other chimpanzees arrived shortly after, gathering at the window and staring wide-eyed at their prodigal community member through the glass. They huddled around the window, except for Dennis, who performed his ritual laps in the background in order to make an impression, as an alpha male leader must do in the chimpanzee world. Julius seemed unafraid as he sat gazing at his chimp family for twenty minutes. Edvard and Billy were entranced by the session, which had gone much better than they had predicted.[37]

TALKING CHIMPANZEES

Back at Moseid's house in Vennesla, Julius was becoming a worthy playmate for the two girls. He slept at night in a cardboard box, which was sometimes kept in the bathroom and sometimes on the floor of Edvard and Marit Moseid's bedroom. As soon as he woke up, however, Julius would dart into the girls' room to play. He was physically smaller than his "sisters," but much more advanced in his motor skills. He climbed the curtains in spite of their efforts to deter him. In truth, he needed all of the climbing practice he could get in advance of the day when he would be returned to the chimpanzee group. He enjoyed wrestling and play-fighting, playing tag and racing with Ane and Siv. If they raced, he made absolutely certain no one cheated. He stood on the start line swaying back and forth while waiting for the start signal. Together with Ane—and only with her—he developed his own game: one of them would sit with a stick or piece of grass sticking out of their mouth while the other tried to grab it with their lips. If the stick happened to slip out of Julius's mouth or if he lost the game, he would get very sour-tempered. The girls also taught him how to draw and paint. He was allowed to lie on their beds for hours on end, though always with the rule that he was not permitted to get used to sleeping in a bed or sitting at a table. For the girls, mealtimes were heart-wrenching, as Julius, the family's uncontested center of attention, would be banned from their company only because it was time to eat. Sweets were also against the rules for Julius but he was quick to learn the art of flattery. When the two girls sat on the sofa, watching children's TV with their snacks, he would squeeze between them, place one arm around each and kiss them on the cheeks, melting their hearts and undoing their parents' principles. Somehow, a piece of candy would "fall" onto the floor or a third straw would just happen to appear in the bottle of soda.[38]

It was inevitable; Julius began adopting more and more human behaviors each day. He learned to recognize verbal messages such as "time to eat" or "we're going outside now." He understood their meaning without difficulty and reacted just like any other child. Unlike other children, however, Julius never gave the impression that he was planning to try speaking up for himself. No single word ever passed his lips.

In 1947, a decisive study was conducted to find out whether it was possible to teach chimpanzees to speak. The psychologist Keith Hayes and his wife, Cathy Hayes, adopted a one-month-old chimpanzee infant named Viki and raised her as a human child with intensive language training. When Viki died at six years of age, she had only learned to say and use four words: "papa," "mama," "cup" and "up." Later studies determined that due to differences in tongue motor skills, it is impossible for chimpanzees to create many of the sounds required for human speech. In 1966, however, the researcher couple, Allen and Beatrice Gardner, was able to teach the chimp Washoe, who lived with them, to communicate using several gestures taken from ASL, or American Sign Language. By the time Washoe left the couple in 1970 to become a part of Roger Fouts's research at the Institute for Primate Studies in Oklahoma, she had mastered 130 different signs.[39] The experiment was hugely significant, suddenly allowing for a relatively advanced method of communication between humans and chimpanzees. Washoe was observed teaching the signs to an adopted chimpanzee son. The following year, inspired by the Gardners' breakthrough, several other chimpanzees were taught ASL. Research with these chimps showed that they were able to group differing objects under the same concept, for example grouping various types of dogs under the term "dog" and various insects under the term "insect." They could transfer signs that they had learned correctly in one context into other contexts. For instance, Washoe had learned the sign for "to open" in the context of a door, but could apply it herself to other situations, such as when she wished to open a crate. And chimps were able to combine different signs into meaningful combinations. Washoe signed the gestures for "water" and "bird" when she saw a swan for the first time. Another chimpanzee combined the signs for "cry" and "fruit" when explaining the concept of an onion.[40]

Although these experiments were well known by the time Julius was born, and though it was apparent that he was able to comprehend quite a lot, there was no point in teaching him sign language communication. On the contrary, the goal for Julius was that he would come to understand and remember that he was a chimpanzee and not a human. Of course, psychologically and commercially it may have been an intriguing idea to raise him the opposite way in order to see just how human-like he could possibly become. Such experiments had been carried out many times in the past. In 1931, the renowned American psychologist Winthrop Niles Kellogg adopted Gua, a seven-month-old chimpanzee, and raised him together with his own ten-month-old son, Donald—in principle providing both youngsters with an identical upbringing. The experiment was called off after only nine months due to Kellogg's disappointment over the chimp's lack of verbal development, but also because he and his wife had begun to realize the danger and unpredictability of certain situations for their human son. A more stalwart couple, Jane and Maurice Temerlin, raised the female chimpanzee Lucy in their home from 1964 until 1976, from the time the chimp was a single day old until she reached the age of twelve. She slept in a crib at their bedside, was fed human formula from a bottle and received care and bodily contact around the clock. At the age of one, she ate meals with the couple at the table, using silverware and a glass just like a human. She often accompanied her mother to work. She never got used to using the toilet, however, nor did she develop the taboo relationship that most humans have to their own feces. At the age of three, she was so difficult to have in the house that the couple was forced to create a separate room for her where she could play without destroying things while unattended. Still, the Termerlins continued their human childrearing. Lucy learned how to dress herself, though she preferred to dress up in other people's clothes rather than her own. She also learned to handle a range of instruments and appliances, from keys and pencils to vacuum cleaners and lighters. She was trained in ASL, and the Temerlins were able to communicate with her in a meaningful way. Lucy loved leafing through newspapers with her own cup of coffee, alongside her parents in the morning. Her coffee was, of course, nothing but warm milk mixed with a teaspoon of coffee to give it color. At only three years of age, she tasted her first sip of alcohol when, by chance, she suddenly grabbed a whiskey glass from a guest who was visiting and chugged it down. When they later discovered Lucy's penchant for boozing in the garden with rotten apples, her liberal foster parents decided it was time to allow her an indulgent drink every now and then. She was thereafter permitted to have a drink or two before dinner, a gin and tonic in the summer and a whiskey sour or

Jack Daniels with 7-Up in the winter.[41] Lucy relished those evenings curled up on the sofa with her parents, sipping her drink and flipping through magazines before dinnertime. When she reached puberty, they gave her a copy of *Playgirl,* which she seemed to enjoy very much. She taught herself to masturbate shamelessly, quite creatively, with the family vacuum cleaner.

For twelve years Lucy's lived like this, but thereafter, things were no longer manageable. It became impossible to have her in the house. Although the chimpanzee is a human's closest genetic relative, it is nonetheless an animal we have never been able to fully tame. Even a chimpanzee hand-raised among humans with familiar, close and emotional bonds will, at some point in time, transform from a tame and predictable animal to a dangerous one. To tame an animal, the species must be systematically bred with particular care to their unique abilities. Modern animal keepers have found it challenging enough to get chimpanzees to breed in captivity; they haven't yet reached the conclusive ability of taming them. Most of the animals that humans have successfully tamed, such as dogs, sheep, goats, pigs, cows and horses, were domesticated over 6,000 years ago.[42]

The Temerlins had put themselves—and Lucy—into an impossible bind. Maurice Temerlin was a psychology professor and the adoption had been part of a larger research project led by the psychologist, Bill Lemmon, in which different types of animals were raised among humans. But the experiment was poorly thought out, morally dubious and completely lacking in a long term plan for the next phase of Lucy's life.[43] The couple didn't want to euthanize her or send her to a zoo or research laboratory, and so the twelve-year-old chimpanzee accompanied researcher Janis Carter to a rehabilitation center for chimpanzees in the Gambia. Carter hoped to persuade Lucy to adapt to a life in the wild. But Lucy was incapable of interacting with other chimpanzees, for example, only becoming sexually aroused by humans. She displayed many of the classic signs of depression, refused to eat for long periods and constantly signed the ASL sign for "pain." After many years of training and acclimation, she was nevertheless set free into the wild. Her skeleton was found two years later, missing its hands and with its head torn off from the rest of the body.[44]

Julius was going to avoid this fate. He was not ever going to sit sipping a gin and tonic with a newspaper in one hand. He was to understand, at all times, his place as a chimpanzee. He was going to be returned to his community.

MOSEID IS PUNISHED

During the summer holiday of 1980, Julius accompanied the Glad family on vacation to Skjern Island outside of Mandal. He was allowed to roam freely around the island, though he never wandered far from Reidun's sight. He preferred sitting on a lounge chair or holding her legs as she worked in the potato patch, playing in the grass with the boys, greeting the neighbor farmer and his sheep, going to the lighthouse in Ryvingen and taking boat trips to the southern rock island archipelagos. People were astonished to see a chimpanzee on a boat. It's hard not to be smitten by a clothed chimp going fishing, and the regional newspaper, *Fædrelandsvennen*, picked up the story. On August 9, 1980, an article was included in the newspaper, written by journalist Trygve Bj. Klingsheim with accompanying photographs by Arild Jakobsen. This article was the first hint at the media storm that Julius would soon unleash. Klingsheim interviewed the four "foster parents," Edvard and Marit Moseid and Billy and Reidun Glad, focusing, among other things, on how the two couples were going to miss him when he was finally returned to his community. The men acted tough and the women were honest.

"It will be a fantastic victory for me. That is when we will know that we were successful," said Edvard Moseid.

"I feel confident that I will be emotionally strong enough to handle it. He is an animal," said Billy Glad.

"I try not to think about it. No, I don't think that I will ever be able to distance myself from him emotionally," admitted Reidun Glad.[45]

Edvard Moseid was often in touch with Elisabeth Nergaard from the TV station NRK, which had filmed several school programs at the zoo. Moseid realized the media potential for the story and told her about Julius. With her interest piqued, she decided to create a television program about the chimp. NRK traveled south with a camera crew to follow the unique, everyday life of Julius. They filmed his participation in the Moseid family chores and captured him on camera dangling from the vacuum handle and splashing in a bucket of suds. This made for good TV, even if it wasn't exactly representative of everyday life in the Moseid home.

Marit Moseid studied during the day. The girls didn't go to daycare but instead accompanied Julius each day to the zoo. This was as good a daycare as any for the girls, and for Julius, it was an essential reminder of his origins as well as his eventual destination. Julius loved the car ride from Vennesla to the zoo. He especially enjoyed holding onto the steering wheel and even managed to figure out that something or other had to be done with his right hand on the stick shift. Moseid had provided a hammock for Julius in his office, but he was allowed to run around as he wished. The girls often took him out around the park, and Edvard took him to see other animals whenever there was time. For the short period that he had been a part of the zoo's chimpanzee community, Julius had only ever spent time in the indoor Tropical House. But in the summer, the chimpanzees were allowed to range freely across a hanging bridge of trees to a large, natural "Chimp Island" with pine trees and bilberry bushes. In his homemade human clothes, diapers and underwear, he crawled around with turtles and rabbits, and got to peer over at Chimp Island toward his parents and fellow species. Edvard noticed that Julius started to get anxious and afraid whenever they neared the island, sometimes putting his hands over Moseid's eyes and grasping tightly onto his neck.[46] Julius's reaction was worrisome. One day, one of the keepers ferried Julius on a small rowboat across the moat toward Chimp Island, while the other chimpanzees were kept inside. But he became so afraid that he wouldn't let go of his keeper.

These distanced meetings with the other chimpanzees were intended to serve a dual purpose. Not only was Julius supposed to remember the other chimps, they also needed to remember him. Edvard Moseid often brought some of Julius's diapers with him to the zoo in order to familiarize the community with the scent. Moseid would pass the diaper to Dennis through the fence, and Dennis would often sit solemnly sniffing his son's feces before handing the diaper off to the other inquisitive chimps.

On Sunday, August 17, 1980, Edvard took Julius into the Tropical House to let the other chimps see him and smell his diaper. He intended to be quick about it because his daughters were waiting in the car. His daughters had asked him to go into the kitchen next to the chimpanzees and get them some fruit. He decided to use the opportunity to display Julius to the other chimps for a moment.

Edvard was behind the public viewing area, in the private sleeping quarters designated for the chimpanzees. The cages were open and he squatted down holding Julius toward the bars so the chimpanzees could see and smell him. Meanwhile, zookeeper Åse Gunn Mosvold was at work in the neighboring kitchen. Several of the chimpanzees had gathered near the bars of the cage. The alpha male Dennis was still outside in the common enclosure, but he suddenly stormed in, visibly agitated. He darted straight over to Moseid, grabbed hold of Julius through the bars, yanked him out of Moseid's arms and pulled him toward the bars. Julius was too big to fit through the bars and so was being squeezed forcefully up against them. Dennis was set to kill his son until Edvard leaned inside the cage, and punched Dennis in the head with all his might. Dennis released Julius and he fell to the floor. In return, however, Dennis grabbed Moseid's arm and now held it in a tight grip. "Get Julius! Get Julius!" Moseid screamed. Mosvold ran over to scoop up the terrified chimpanzee. Julius was safe, but now Dennis was refusing to release Moseid's arm. Mosvold tried desperately to loosen his grip on Edvard, kicking the bars and Dennis's hand. Edvard tried to hit Dennis with his free arm, but Dennis wouldn't let go. Edvard was afraid the chimpanzee would tear his arm off, something he was physically capable of doing, but Dennis seemed to be most interested in his hand. Edvard clenched his fist as hard as he could, but it wasn't difficult for Dennis to pry open the fist, finger by finger. Dennis took his time, like a torturer who knows that the waiting and fearful anticipation are more traumatic for the victim than any actual pain. The girls meanwhile were waiting outside in the car, wondering what could be taking their father so long. After Dennis had pried Edvard's index finger open, he looked at it before sticking it into his mouth and biting it clean off with his razor sharp canine teeth. Edvard howled in shock and pain, Dennis released his hold, and both Moseid and Mosvold fell over backward onto the floor.[47]

In the same way that Dennis, or possibly one of the other chimps, had bitten off one of Julius's fingers earlier that year, Dennis had punished and humiliated Edvard according to chimpanzee etiquette, by biting off a finger. Mosvold saw the bone protruding straight out of Moseid's skin. Edvard rushed around madly, looking for a piece of paper towel to wrap around his hand. Mosvold insisted that someone drive him to the hospital immediately, but Moseid refused, claiming it would be better to first drop his daughters off at their grandparents' house before going to the doctor. Once in his car, however, the blood drained from his face and he felt dizzy. He finally gave in and allowed someone to drive him to the West Agder Central Hospital.

Julius and Edvard had each lost part of a finger. Like an ironic version of Michelangelo's *The Creation of Adam*, they could now point at one another with their bitten-off fingertips. They were now marked for life and forever bound together.

Chapter 3

A ROOM OF ONE'S OWN

"A chimpanzee kept in solitude
is not a real chimpanzee at all."[48]

WOLFGANG KÖHLER

D URING JULIUS'S EARLY life, most of our knowledge about
wild chimpanzees came from a single human: the British
researcher Jane Goodall. Since childhood, Goodall had
dreamed of moving to Africa and living among the chimpanzees. She chanced upon just such an opportunity in adulthood
when a former schoolmate moved to a farm in Kenya and
invited Jane to visit. Once in Kenya, Jane first landed a job
as a secretary in Nairobi. However, her interest in chimpanzees eventually led her to cross paths with National Museum
paleontologist and anthropologist, Louis Leakey. He was so
impressed with the self-taught Jane Goodall that he soon hired
her as his own secretary. Leakey allowed Jane to accompany
him as he searched for the fossils of prehistoric human species while at the same time putting her skills as a field worker

to the test. He was persuaded by what he saw and suggested that Goodall carry out a pioneering study in Tanzania following the wild chimpanzees in the Gombe National Park on Lake Tanganyika over a long period. Her work would provide the research community with the first ever glimpse into the daily lives of wild chimpanzees. The fact that Goodall was self-taught and unschooled on the subject was more of a boon than a disadvantage, Leakey believed. He would secure financial funding, but she would have to find a partner to join her endeavors. On July 16, 1960, Goodall left for a four-month-long research trip together with her mother, Vanna, and a local cook named Dominic.[49]

The project was both audacious and naïve. Goodall was twenty-six years old, inexperienced, petite, beautiful and blonde. She intended to go around unprotected with her notebook and binoculars in an area populated by wild chimpanzees, leopards, snakes and buffalos. Several weeks passed before she observed a single thing. Both she and her mother came down with serious cases of malaria. But after three months of fieldwork, she made a groundbreaking discovery as the first human ever to observe the use of tools between wild chimpanzees. Leakey had been searching for just such a breakthrough and had explained to her beforehand that an observation like this would justify the entire project. For the first time, Goodall observed and described the manner in which the chimpanzees selected sticks, modified them by removing leaves and adjoining twigs and then proceeded to use them to fish termites out of hollow tree stumps—in other words, the chimps created and used tools. The implications were far-reaching, not only for how one viewed chimpanzees, but also for the very definition of what it means to be human: "Now we must redefine tool, redefine Man, or accept chimpanzees as humans," Leakey responded by telegraph after receiving news of the discovery.[50] Up until then, humans had been defined as the only creature to use tools, a tone set by the 1949 Kenneth Oakley classic, *Man the Tool-Maker*. From now on, what it meant to be human would have to be redefined. Goodall's breakthrough led to renewed funding and an extended period of research work in the field.

After the chimpanzees realized that the strange white female primate with binoculars was no threat to them, Jane Goodall was slowly able to come into closer quarters with them. She began recognizing each one individually and gave them names. She learned to decode the various forms of body language between the chimpanzees, many of them strikingly similar to human gestures such as kissing and embracing, holding hands or patting one another on the shoulder for encouragement. She discovered several ways in which the chimpanzees used tools, such as their tendency to pick leaves and then proceed to chew and crumple them up so that they would become soft and absorbent and useful as sponges to retrieve water from difficult-to-reach holes in tree trunks. Or how they would crack nuts with an assortment of objects, or use leaves to clean themselves off when dirty. The male chimpanzees, in particular, would wash away their semen directly after mating. Goodall eventually got so close to the chimpanzees that she was allowed to touch them, to stroke and groom their fur and to feed them from her hand. Of course, this was extremely risky behavior—the chimpanzees were also at risk of catching contagious diseases to which they were not immune—but Goodall had both faith in God and a solid dose of luck and survived these experiences. She was able to come into closer contact with chimpanzees than any other human before her, in part due to a banana feeding station, which she established in her camp beginning in 1963. This method later received heavy criticism because it influenced and altered the community's behavior. However, the station made it possible for Goodall to observe how cunning the chimpanzees could be in securing the largest possible number of bananas for themselves. One of the chimpanzees named Figan managed to dupe the others in his group multiple times by pretending to have caught the scent of a promising food source in the forest. He lured the other chimpanzees to investigate the scent with him before abandoning the search party and sneaking back to Goodall's camp where he knew there would be bananas he could enjoy all to himself.[51] In another situation, Goodall set up an experiment in which she placed bananas in boxes that could be opened with a screw and a nut, provided the chimpanzees were able to learn the system. Some of them were successful; others were not. One of the chimps was able to figure out the system quickly and learned to hide his abilities from the others in the group. He would wait until the others were looking in the opposite direction before discreetly opening the box with the screw. After that, he would sit nonchalantly with one hand on the lid without giving off any indication that he had been able to open the lock, all the time waiting until the others would give up and go away so he could eat his bananas in peace.

National Geographic sent the photographer Hugo van Lawick to the Gombe to document the fascinating interplay between the plucky researcher, Goodall, and the wild chimpanzees. The result was a storybook ending. The photographer and Goodall fell in love, married and had a child who was sometimes kept safe in a small cage in the jungle so the chimpanzees wouldn't kidnap him. In addition, Goodall's fame grew through a series of magazine reports and her research project became a permanent research center, formally established as the Jane Goodall Institute in 1977. At the center, students and scientists could now follow the lives of individual chimpanzees over decades and generations and thus gather a uniquely vast amount of information about the life cycle of a community of wild chimpanzees. Among other studies, these researchers have followed thirteen young chimpanzees that had experienced, like Julius, separation from their mothers at a young age. The researchers were able to monitor these chimps until adulthood to observe the course of their lives and well-being. Most of these chimpanzees experienced what Goodall labeled "clinical depression," displaying signs of apathy and a notably low frequency of mating. Some of them died because they were not able to take care of themselves without their mothers. Others experienced long-lasting changes in behavior, while still others adjusted to normal chimpanzee behavior after a while.

Edvard Moseid and Billy Glad, who had both read everything Jane Goodall had written, hoped that Julius would land in this last category. Thus far, there was nothing to indicate that Julius suffered from any form of depression. At the same time, it was very unclear what now needed to happen in order to return him to his mother and the rest of the chimpanzee group at the zoo. Many of the zoo staff thought it completely

unrealistic to return Julius back to his community. They
believed Moseid and Glad were refusing to see reality because
they were blinded by their feelings for the small animal. Of
course, the skeptics were right.

THE CAGE PROCEDURE

The pain in Edvard Moseid's finger did not let up after Dennis's brutal attack. On August 29, 1980, Moseid was once again
taken to the West Agder Central Hospital, and Julius was sent
back to the Glad family for a few days. Now that Julius had
grown, he was able to join in more advanced forms of play
with the Glad sons, Carl Christian and Øystein. They had
a cowboy-themed Playmobil setup, complete with a sheriff,
saloon, horses and people figures that they would set up on the
floor, improvising the figures' movements and dialogue. Julius,
who had a tendency to clamber through the buildings and people, toppling the whole setup, earned the name "King-Kong."[52]

Glad worried that Julius was inspired by the two children
to walk around on his hind legs. And he realized that Julius
was being raised much more freely than Billy, the other young
zoo chimpanzee. Billy would never dream of eating a banana
or apple until he had looked at his mother Lotta and received a
confirming glance that it was all right. It was hard to imagine
Julius adapting to these kinds of social graces once he rejoined
the chimpanzee group. At the same time, it was difficult to
figure out how the chimpanzee mothers were able to extract
such obedience and discipline from their young. Marit Moseid
would often stand by, watching the interaction between Lotta
and Billy in the hopes of learning the key to such motherly

behavior so she might implement it with Julius. But she was unable to crack the code.[53]

Edvard Moseid and Billy Glad agreed that, from here on out, they would all need to be stricter with Julius and ensure that he only ran around on four legs. In order to set boundaries for Julius, they decided to experiment with a method of biting him on the neck and arms when necessary. They tried to bite somewhat strongly with the knowledge that he would have to get used to the strong bites of other chimpanzees once he returned to the community. Billy Glad once bit Julius hard enough that he knew his own sons would have screamed in pain from it. Julius, however, simply gave him a playful smile.[54]

Physically, Julius was developing nicely. At nine months old, he weighed 16.5 pounds, his coat was glossy and clean and smelled good, his teeth were fine and his motor skills impressive—at least as compared to a human child.[55] His motor skills were so impressive, in fact, that it was starting to be challenging to have him in a human home. The two families sent him back and forth between their houses. For most of August and all of September, he lived in Vennesla; at the start of October he spent several weeks with the Glads in Bliksheia. Both households did their best to clean up and make repairs when he was away. Julius was now able to climb up and open cupboard doors whenever he liked. He made a mess in the kitchens, discovered paint cans in the Moseid family cellar and spilled paint all over the stairs. Each time before Julius returned, Billy and Reidun Glad tried to limit the potential damage by closing off rooms in the house that they didn't want ruined, as well as by removing plants and other loose objects in the rooms where he was allowed to roam.

Finally, toward the end of October 1980, a room was set up for Julius at the zoo. That is to say, the entire chimpanzee facility was reorganized so that from here on out, three fixed sleeping areas were designated for the chimpanzees, one of which was reserved for Julius. These quarters were closed to the public. The chimpanzees entered the cages by way of a shutter door that would be opened for them. For as long as Julius was in one of the cages alone, he could not see but only hear and smell the other chimpanzees when they were in the two other cages. The plan was for Julius to spend as much time as possible in this space. In this way, he and the other chimpanzees would gradually get used to one another. The cage was a few square yards in size, with red bars, some straw on the floor and a climbing rope dangling from the top. Julius was allowed to take off his diaper and human clothes as soon as he was in the cage, but one of Edvard Moseid's jackets was placed inside as a small scent memory from the human world.

Julius would first have to learn to be by himself in the cage. After some time, he then would begin to stay the night. Glad saw this relocation as the definitive milestone in Julius's reintegration. "If he (and we) are able to carry this off, the chances in respect to his future are relatively positive. If he is not able, then what we have is an enormous problem on our hands, one that can hardly result in anything other than euthanasia," he reflected.[56] However, to pull this off was emotionally challenging. Both of the families were required to let go and gradually lose contact with this being whom they had grown to love. If the so-called cage procedure were to succeed, they would have to be systematic and united in their efforts. They established a "rehabilitation team" consisting of Billy Glad,

Edvard Moseid and the two zookeepers, Grete Svendsen and Jakob Kornbrekke. The first time they brought Julius to the cage, he was only to stay for a little while and would be given something to eat inside the cage in order to build positive associations. And in order to contain Dennis's reactions, they decided to medicate Dennis with Valium whenever Julius was in the cage. It was Dennis they feared more than anything. Julius could not expect any special sort of protection from Dennis just because he was his biological son. Fatherhood is not a significant relationship in the chimpanzee world. As the alpha male, Dennis was primarily responsible for keeping things peaceful and orderly. He could quickly turn violent if Julius were to return to the group and misbehave.

On October 29, 1980, along with Edvard, Julius spent time in the cage for the first time. His reaction to the new surroundings was surprisingly positive. Dennis responded well on the Valium and didn't show any irritation over his new neighbor, while the other chimpanzees displayed curiosity and interest in Julius. Over the next days, Julius returned with the Moseid girls who played with him inside his cage. But on October 31, he had an accident on his climbing rope. He fell against the bars and hurt one of his front teeth. The tooth was so badly damaged that it had to be pulled. Ørnulf Nandrup, the dentist, came to the zoo on November 6, and Glad set up an improvised operation room in Moseid's office. Julius was put under anesthesia, and within seven minutes Nandrup had pulled out the entire tooth, which proved to have a much longer root than a human baby tooth. Julius began to wake up fifteen minutes after the operation and only a half hour later was in the Glad family car on his way home to recuperate.[57] He was limp and behaved oddly in the car, but after they arrived, he soon calmed down on Reidun's lap and slept through the entire night.

The next day, however, he was still behaving strangely. He seemed tired, wobbly on his legs, and confused. He was given a bit of Valium and had to take a long nap next to Billy on the bathroom floor. On November 8, he still wasn't himself and was given more Valium. This recovery period led to a prolonged interruption to the cage procedure, an interruption in which Julius once again got to be human. This might explain why the project got off to a bad start the second time around. Julius was fine as long as there were people nearby, but as soon as he was left alone in the cage, he began to howl and scream. On one day, he was left alone in the cage for six hours, five of them spent screaming. Grete Svendsen was worn out from having to work under such conditions, so the team decided that in the future Julius would be given two daily doses of 5 milligrams of Valium to calm him. His father Dennis was put on a double dose to deal with the stress of having Julius close by.[58] Father and son were separated by mesh cages and both were heavily medicated so they could tolerate each other's presence.

THE FIRST NIGHT IN THE CAGE

The whole process was messy and confusing for Julius. For the time being, he lived in Vennesla in the evenings and overnight, but spent his days in the cage at the zoo. He was a human by night and a chimpanzee by day. For five- and three-year-old Ane and Siv Moseid, it was hard to understand why Julius was being forced to sit alone and afraid in a cage for so many hours a day when it was obvious that he loved being with them. On November 18, Julius became hysterical when he was put into the cage, baring his teeth at Edvard, howling constantly and only stopping when he was taken out again. The cage procedure had reached a complete standstill. The team resolved to be firm and consistent, keeping him in the cage even if he howled, though one of them was allowed to sit inside with him for up to two hours a day in order to ensure his safety.[59] And on December 3, 1980, the day—or rather the night—finally came when Julius was scheduled to spend his first night in the cage. Julius gave Edvard his most pitiful look once he realized he was going to be left alone. As Moseid turned off the light and went home for the evening, he could hear Julius's sobs in the dark cage.[60]

It was hard for people to drift off to sleep in Vennesla that night. Emotionally, Julius was a kind of younger brother to the Moseid sisters. They couldn't imagine any other way of categorizing him. And you don't put your brother into a cage. They were angry with their dad. How could he do something so pointlessly hurtful to someone they loved so much? For Marit Moseid, the process was no less challenging than for her two daughters. After all, she had been the one to carry out the bulk of the daily responsibilities regarding Julius. She and Julius had developed a very close bond, and he was now like a third child in the family. While he had lived at their home, she had changed Julius's diapers, as she had for both Ane and Siv, bathed all three children, fed them in the evenings, brushed their teeth and put them to bed. And now suddenly, her youngest was sent off to live in a cage. She found it hard to think about it in a professional context. For Edvard Moseid, the zoo director who was frequently required to make tough decisions about various animals, the situation was not quite as awful. But even he didn't find it easy.

No one knows how Julius fared that night, what time he calmed down, and when he finally fell asleep. When his keepers came in the next morning, they found that he had broken his other front tooth during the night, perhaps from crying with a gaping mouth and then throwing himself against the floor or bars. Nandrup had to be called in again. The operation went well, but Julius continued to harm himself. He bled from his mouth every day, Grete Svendsen noted. Was he deliberately trying to hurt himself? Those on his rehabilitation team speculated whether or not he intended to inflict self-harm.[61] They were at a loss. The cage procedure was going so badly that they considered skipping it altogether. Should they jump straight into the next phase: introducing Julius to the community? Such an introduction would be very risky, of course. Dennis was a threat and several of the other chimpanzees appeared to have lost patience with the howling guest next door.

The rehabilitation team voted to introduce Julius to a selected chimp, and chose the five-year-old female, Bølla. She was the right gender and the right age. She was also the one who had previously cared so much for Julius the first time he was rejected by Sanne. The team decided first to test the effects of the calming agent Vallergan on Julius for a few days after which they planned to give Bølla Rohypnol to put her to sleep and then present Julius to the sleeping female.

On December 15, 1980, Bølla was taken out and isolated from the other chimpanzees, but things did not go according to the plan. The original idea was to sedate her through her food but separation from the other chimps made her so angry and uneasy that Bølla refused to eat. Meanwhile, Julius raged inside his cage, howling with his jaw stretched wide and exposing his two missing front teeth. He tried flinging himself against the bars, but Moseid had padded them with plastic to keep him from harming himself. Because Bølla refused to take her sedatives through food, they had to lead her unmedicated into the room alongside Julius's cage. The veterinarian Gudbrand Hval brought another medication that could be administered through a blowpipe, and the new plan was to sedate her with the blowpipe in the cage. However, she became so remarkably calm in the presence of Julius that both Moseid and Glad were at once struck by the same thought: What if they tried putting both chimps together without sedatives? What would happen if they opened the shutter door, leaving both Julius and Bølla alone together?

They decided to take a chance and opened the shutter. Bølla could now go in to Julius and Julius could go out to Bølla. Edvard's and Billy's eyes were fixed on every move. Bølla was the one to finally take initiative. She calmly made her way in to Julius's cage. He howled, but was much less hysterical than Glad and Moseid had expected. Bølla surprised them and acted gently and curiously rather than being threatening or scary. She reached out to Julius and he quieted down. When Julius once again began to howl, Bølla reacted by being strict, rattling his bed until he became quiet again. Then they both went into the larger cage together. Julius provoked Bølla by assuming a fight position, but Bølla took it as playfulness and did not let herself be drawn in. Billy Glad believed

Dennis would instantly have killed Julius for attempting such a stance.

At 2:25 p.m., they touched. For the first time in almost a year, Julius once again had physical contact with a member of his own species. At three o'clock, their play became more heated, so Moseid and Glad decided to separate them. The separation went well. When each of them was in their own cage, the door between them was shut. Bølla was allowed to rejoin the other chimpanzees and was fortunately spared any kind of punishment for being outside of the group with Julius. Julius accompanied Edvard home to Vennesla.

The next day, Bølla and Julius were placed together again, this time for a half hour. In the evening, Glad came to visit Julius after he was back safely in his own cage. Julius was allowed to come out and interact with him and several other keepers before Glad had to return him to his cage. Once inside, Julius sat sucking his thumb and thinking. Glad thought that Julius looked pensive. "Maybe he's sitting there pondering and starting to understand that he perhaps isn't a human after all," Glad speculated that evening.[62]

Could Glad be right? Could Julius, in fact, be speculating about what he was? Chimpanzees are among the few species of animals with the ability to self-reflect. Studies have shown that most mammals—with the exception of chimpanzees, orangutans and humans—have difficulties in understanding the concept of mirrors. Other mammal species are tempted to try grabbing the individual they see in the mirror, to walk behind the mirror to look for the creature, or they are frightened by the strange "other" animal. The American psychologist Gordon Gallup conducted a clever experiment in the 1970s in which various animals received a mark on their foreheads without realizing it and were thereafter confronted with a mirror. Chimpanzees, orangutans and human children, eighteen months or older, noticed the mark in the mirror. They touched their own foreheads with their hands, trying to understand what it was and to wipe it off; in other words, they understood that the reflections in the mirror were themselves. Other animals and younger children did not grasp the connection. These three species possess a mental capacity that is rare in the animal world, one marked by the ability to be aware of and recognize one's self.[63]

There's nothing particularly surprising about the chimpanzee's ability to recognize itself in a mirror. The entire social etiquette around which a chimpanzee community is structured is built upon the self-awareness of each member. Each chimp is aware of how the others perceive it and how its own behavior is interpreted by the others, as well as how to behave in order to reach a desired outcome. Chimpanzees display fear by exposing both their upper and lower teeth. In conflict situations in which it is beneficial to appear fearless, researchers have observed chimpanzees' feverish and mostly futile attempts to hide their fear responses with their hands. Frans de Waal described how, Luit, a male chimpanzee in the Arnhem zoo, pulled his lips together with his hands in order to hide his teeth and fear response from his rival. Luit didn't succeed at first, though, and was instead overcome by fear, exposing his teeth, but he continued to try pulling his lips together again. Only on his third attempt was he able to discipline his face enough so that he could go out in the open and swagger about like a tough guy in front of his chimpanzee rival.[64] A highly developed sense of self-awareness is thus vital to a chimpanzee's survival. When the chimpanzee Washoe learned to sign in ASL, she was the first chimpanzee in the world to put this self-awareness into words. As she gazed at her own reflection, she was asked "Who that?" and quickly answered the sign for "Me Washoe."[65] In a different experiment Viki, another chimpanzee raised among humans, was given a pile of photographs featuring humans and animals and asked to sort them. She quite correctly separated them into two piles, one of the humans and one of all the animals. She made only one mistake, though not perhaps from her perspective, she placed the photograph of herself into the pile with the human photos.[66]

No one can say into which pile Julius would have placed himself. It was no easy task for Julius to figure out whether he was animal or human. Up until this point he had been a bit of both; he was almost chimpanzee, almost human.

Chapter 4

HOME FOR CHRISTMAS

*"Julius to spend Christmas
among his own kind."* [67]
FÆDRELANDSVENNEN NEWSPAPER

I N THE MIDST of the turbulent cage-training process, on December 1, 1980, the NRK channel premiered the program that Elisabeth Nergaard had produced about Julius. The feature episode was twenty-two minutes long and was first broadcast on the children's TV program and later repeated multiple times on the so-called school television programming during the daytime. In 1980, most Norwegians only had access to this one channel, so the majority of Norwegian children soon developed a relationship with the charming chimpanzee. The concept was particularly well suited for children's television, since it was easy for children to identify with a chimpanzee in diapers who crawled around and played with his "siblings." The whole country watched Julius do chores, scrub the floor with soapsuds on his chin, climb the curtains, paint and draw with the Moseid girls and build Playmobil structures with the Glad boys.

There was little doubt that Norwegian children wanted more of Julius. He had suddenly become the country's most beloved animal. Elisabeth Nergaard had already started working on a new episode, which was to feature Julius's first birthday party at the Moseid home with the Glad brothers, Carl Christian and Øystein, as party guests. There was something artificial and untimely about the birthday party. At the time that the second episode was being filmed, Julius was in reality in the midst of his strict cage procedure and was spending his nights at the zoo, though the NRK program made it appear as though he was still roaming about the Moseid household like a member of the family in human clothes. Still, it made for good television.

For his birthday party, the table was set with Christmas decorations, and for once, Julius was allowed to sit at the table. He was served soda and a cake inscribed with "Julius 1 Year." He was dressed in diapers, underpants and a T-shirt. The commercial details were well attended to. His T-shirt bore an advertisement for the zoo, and the brand of his diapers were those of a sponsor.[68] The Glad brothers brought a present, of course. Julius ran to them as they came up the stairs and threw himself onto Øystein's chest. Carl Christian helped him to open the gift, a little toy monkey that Julius completely ignored. The girls gave him a toy drum set with drumsticks that he soon began to enjoy.

They sang happy birthday in English, and Julius sat at the end of the table and received the first slice of cake. "Let's see whether Julius will get married someday," Edvard Moseid said, referring to a Norwegian superstition in which a slice of cake that remains upright on a plate signals a happy love life and a fallen slice, by contrast, a lonesome fate. "Oh, no! Bummer, there she falls!" Moseid had to admit when, despite his most careful efforts with the cake knife, Julius's slice fell onto its side on the plate. Julius didn't seem to care about the cake. He picked off some of the chocolate decorations but made more of a mess than anything else. He sat quietly and seemed confused at the table, moving slowly and calmly and poking at the icing with his fingers. The children had to look on in disappointment as most of the cake was ruined and unappetizing after Julius smeared the icing around.[69]

The journalist, Trygve Bj. Klingsheim, and photographer, Arild Jakobsen, who had published the first news story about Julius, were now planning a children's book about him. On March 8, 1981, Reidun and Billy Glad went to visit Edvard and Marit Moseid for a photo session with Julius for the book.[70] Julius was photographed playing in the snow, sitting on toboggan and wearing a pale blue hat inside of a sheepskin sleeping bag that the Moseid girls had grown out of. The photo shoot served to illustrate the schizophrenic nature of the situation. Julius was in limbo. He spent his nights in his zoo cage and much of the daytime with Bølla, but then he would suddenly be fetched and dressed up like a human child. Glad noted that Julius had started to smell like a zoo animal living in an enclosure, though he was still tame and familiar with his human home as in his earlier days.[71] He had become physically and hygienically more animal-like, but was still socially and emotionally quite human.

The zoo was in a bit of a bind. On one hand, the focus should have been fully on Julius's reintegration into his community with every follow-up action devoted solely to this aim. On the other hand by the summer of 1981, Julius had become the zoo's main attraction. The television success had changed everything. And the zoo was, after all, a commercial institution, and Julius was still small and tame enough that visitors were able to meet him in person. Edvard couldn't keep himself from capitalizing on this somewhat. Julius was therefore appointed as a zoo "guide." Visitors could accompany him around the zoo and watch him introduce the other animals, ending their unorthodox tour by receiving an autograph of sorts from Julius on a scrap of paper. "It can be somewhat problematic when the tour guide himself is more of an attraction than what he is supposed to be presenting," wrote the newspaper *VG* after attending one of Julius's famous tours.[72]

At the same time, Julius's keepers were working on assimilating Julius with the other chimpanzees. By this point, Julius had spent a lot of time with Bølla in the sleeping quarter cages. In this behind-the-scenes area, the zookeepers could easily reach in through the bars of the cages if anything were to happen. In the fall of 1981, they decided that they would introduce Julius in person to the other chimpanzees inside the large, open indoor facility in the Tropical House. Long preparations were made leading up to the anticipated meeting, as it was to be a critical point in the reintegration process. The facility was designed like an artificial mountain, with a small rocky formation with tree trunks and climbing ropes facing a moat and the zoo's visitors. Julius was often brought here to play and Ane and Siv had accompanied him on occasion. In this way, he was able to become familiar with the installations and climbing trees and to learn to be cautious around the moat. The keepers planned to put him in with Bølla, Lotta and Billy in November of 1981.

NRK returned to film a new episode for the series, a natural conclusion to the trilogy in which Julius was expected to be safely reunited with the world of chimpanzees. But the reintegration was anything but safe. Edvard did not have a Plan B, nor were any of the zookeepers waiting with hoses to fend off the other chimpanzees in case they might try to grab him. Moseid had convinced himself that everything would go smoothly.[73] NRK gave their word that if the event turned into a fiasco and the adult chimpanzees went loose on Julius and killed him as they had killed Skinny, the news station would not release the footage.

Julius first had to meet Bølla. She was released inside the enclosure alone and afterwards Moseid entered with Julius on his arm. Moseid thereby placed himself into an extremely risky situation, since Bølla was nearly a fully adult female chimpanzee. As Edvard and Julius entered the Tropical House, Bølla climbed up to the highest point. She began marking her territory and yanked aggressively on the rope. Julius refused to let go of Moseid's hand, whining loudly and howling in a pitiful manner.

Even though Bølla and Julius had spent time together inside the cages, the situation devolved to become much more tense and unnerving now that they were meeting in the open. Edvard released Julius, hoping that he would head toward Bølla, but Julius merely screeched and ran back to him. Moseid tried again, but Julius once again sprang back up onto Moseid's arms. Suddenly Moseid realized that Bølla was about to attack him. He had to act quickly, discarding Julius and running out of the chimpanzee area, shutting the door and latching it.

Julius must have felt abandoned once more. At the age of only six weeks old, his mother, Sanne, had abandoned him. And now Edvard Moseid had done the same. Confused, Julius sat at the shut door, crying. Edvard ran out and around to the other side of the exhibit where, along with Marit, he had to observe the rest of the encounter from the public viewpoint across the moat. What they saw was little Julius together with a large, dangerous chimpanzee in an open arena without human authority or control. At first, Julius's cries sounded frightened, but they soon turned into wild screeches. To a human ear, they sounded like purely primal cries. Bølla kept her distance the entire time. The Moseid couple longed for nothing more than to go in and free the young chimp.

Julius continued to yelp and cry, as Bølla gradually grew calmer. It appeared that she had finished marking her territory and was ready to receive him. She tried coming closer to Julius but each time he would move away from her. She remained patient and waited, eventually shifting the interaction. Julius became more interested and began to move in her direction. She sat with an open lap. Julius inched toward her. When he finally reached her, he crawled into her lap and Bølla wrapped her long chimpanzee arms around him and stroked him gently.

Edvard and Marit Moseid were extremely relieved. Instead of killing Julius, Bølla had embraced him. Julius needed comfort and he had sought it in the only available lap. He had communicated correctly; he had displayed his fear and submission, choosing not to challenge her. For these reasons, he had been accepted. Bølla and Julius continued playing and remaining close together. He crawled back into her lap several times and was again given the loving embrace that he so needed.

The next step was to bring in the two dwarf hippos that lived in a different part of the Tropical House but shared the moat with the chimpanzees. The Moseids knew that Julius was afraid of the hippos, but the test was now whether or not he would seek comfort with Bølla when he felt unsafe. This experiment went well, too, and Julius appeared much less afraid of the hippos now that he was getting along with Bølla.

Finally, Edvard decided to bring in both Lotta and little Billy. In human terms, Billy and Julius were half brothers, as they shared Dennis as their father. But in the chimpanzee world, siblings are those who have the same mother, and so Julius and Billy were only nominally related. Though Billy was slightly older than Julius, he was smaller. From a human perspective, Julius would come across as more competent and intelligent than Billy since Julius had picked up on human behaviors that human viewers were better able to understand and recognize. In reality, Billy's motor skills were much more advanced than Julius's. Julius was a clumsy chimpanzee who was bad at climbing and afraid of heights.

Julius was remarkably calm when Lotta and Billy entered the enclosure but now Bølla appeared visibly afraid. Bølla was ranked lower than Lotta and was therefore required to display fear and submissiveness. The two female chimpanzees walked around for a while, each with their young crawling nearby. When the two adults became less watchful, the two young chimps found each other. Suddenly, the brothers sat down and hugged one another. They sat like this for a long time before deciding to explore the pen. Billy was in front as though he wanted to show Julius his world, and Julius followed right behind him with a hand on his older brother's back. After this, Lotta also approached Julius and put her arms around him.[74] It was as though all of them wished to welcome him and offer comfort and love.

THE ALPHA MALE GETS BURNED

The reintegration project was surprisingly successful. Julius was released into the community group and the chimpanzees accepted him. He was able to interact freely in the Tropical House during the day, but for his safety, was kept isolated from the others at night so he could sleep alone. His mother Sanne, however, was completely indifferent to Julius. She acted as though she had no idea who he was. But Julius appeared to get along among the rest of the group despite not having a caring mother. His father, the alpha male Dennis, was still the only chimpanzee who had not yet been put in the enclosure with Julius.

Julius was integrated and yet he was still a strange chimpanzee. It was obvious that he had picked up tendencies and behaviors from his time spent among humans. For example, he would pull straw up over his body like a small blanket before going to sleep. At times he would turn the plastic water bowl upside down and push it around as though it was a toy car. Or he would quite clearly long for his other world and cry and hang on the doorknob that led out to the humans. None of the other chimpanzees would ever imagine behaving in such a way.

In the late fall of 1981, Dennis was released back into the group with Julius, and at first, things seemed to go well. Dennis was a good group leader; he was strict but just. Julius did not pose a threat or rivalry, and Dennis decided to accept this motherless outsider. The zookeepers, however, continued to monitor the chimpanzees carefully whenever both Dennis and Julius were together.[75]

Although Dennis was the uncontested leader of the community, he was not a physically strong alpha male. He would become exhausted and his lips would bleed whenever he had to perform his ritual calls to impress the others and maintain his power. He had a weak heart and had been further weakened and scarred after a large fire that had occurred in the zoo one year before Julius was born. On August 2, 1978, the Tropical House, the zoo's new pride and joy, caught fire. An airplane pilot heading south toward the Kjevik airport had radioed to the control tower that they could see smoke rising from one of the zoo buildings. The control tower contacted the fire station, but by the time two fire trucks and seven men arrived, the Tropical House was already ablaze. Although they were able to control the fire within five minutes, the smoke had spread considerably and the animals were in danger of carbon monoxide poisoning. Edvard Moseid, the veterinarian Gudbrand Hval, Billy Glad and several others assisted in the rescue operations, as did the fire crew and police. Moseid had to decide which animals to prioritize. Most of the snakes and lizards already appeared to be dead, so the crocodiles and chimpanzees took top priority. The crocodiles sought natural protection underwater. In order to get them out, they would first have to drain the water from the pool. The firemen wanted to pump the water out, but one of the keepers voluntarily reached an arm into the pool and yanked out the drain stop while the others warded the crocodiles off with sticks. As soon as the water was gone, the crocodiles were bound and carried out. Of the five chimpanzees that were community members at the time, Bølla had luckily spent the previous night outside on Chimp Island, while the male chimpanzee, Polle, fell into the moat during the fire and drowned. The three remaining chimpanzees, Dennis, Sanne and Lotta, lay unconscious on the floor of the sleeping quarters. The firemen carried them outside of the Tropical House and put them on the ground to be treated just like human smoke inhalation victims. They were lifted into stable sideways positions and given myocardial massages and artificial respiration with smoke diver devices with both oxygen and Cardiazol. The firemen later said it felt like the chimpanzees knew they had come to help them. When the oxygen tube slipped out of one chimpanzee's mouth, he grabbed it and put it back in himself. After over an hour of treatment, they slowly began to wake up. Later in the day, they were taken to Chimp Island. Bølla, who had spent the night alone, was incredibly gentle and comforted the wounded chimpanzees. The other chimps could hardly respond to her gestures. Clearly nauseous and dizzy, they couldn't do anything other than sit in the heather with their faces in their hands. Powerful nausea and intense headaches are among the symptoms experienced by humans suffering from smoke inhalation. The chimpanzees were obviously experiencing the same symptoms. Over the next days, they were given penicillin, diuretics and heart medication dissolved in apple juice. It was August; the nights were warm and so the chimpanzees would be allowed to live outside on Chimp Island for the time being. A temporary shelter was set up for them outside while the Tropical House was quickly rebuilt. Dennis was so weak after the fire that he could hardly push himself up the stairs to the shelter on Chimp Island.[76]

The fire and the subsequent medical treatment marked the point at which Billy Glad, originally the doctor for zoo employees, also took over medical responsibility for the chimpanzees. Humans and chimpanzees are so similar anatomically that it was most likely more beneficial for the chimps to be treated by a human-trained doctor than by a general veterinarian. All three chimpanzees survived, however, Dennis never fully recovered. Now, three years after the fire, the negative effects were plain to see. His heart was weak, and he was easily fatigued.

"CHRISTMAS AMONG HIS OWN KIND"

In the fall of 1981, Julius's mother Sanne began showing signs of pregnancy. Moseid and Glad now interpreted Sanne's previous disinterest in Julius when he had first been reintroduced to the group as an expression of her pregnancy, which they had not realized at the time. Perhaps her motherly interest had been completely occupied by her expected baby.[77] Among chimpanzees, four years usually pass between the time a female gives birth and when she becomes fertile again, but because Sanne had rejected Julius, her milk production had stopped very soon, enabling her to become fertile again much earlier. On December 12, 1981, she bore a male chimpanzee who was named Kjell, after the keeper who had been on guard during his birth. Kjell was an unusual chimpanzee baby due to a skeletal disease that meant he would always be small.[78] But he was much more dogged in hanging on to his mother than Julius had ever been. Sanne once again displayed a lack of motherly instincts, but Kjell was an infant who refused to let go or to accept being put down. He clung to his mother, not only onto her back or stomach as most young chimpanzees do, but also often hanging onto her arms for hours as she walked around the enclosure.

Dennis had become a father once more. This would prove to be the last time. He had gradually grown weaker over the fall. Glad had sedated him to keep him calm, but on December 21, 1981, he went on another dominance display run through the Tropical House. His lips turned bluer than usual, and he stopped to pant for breath. Gudbrand Hval and Billy Glad were summoned and together they lured Dennis into his own room. They quickly put him on heart medication. In addition, they concluded he had now contracted pneumonia. They were able to lessen his pain and help with some of the symptoms, but worried that he might need a heart operation and didn't know whether he could survive being put under anesthesia. The next day his condition took a dramatic turn for the worse. And at 2 p.m., Dennis, the alpha male leader, died.[79]

All of the humans who were with the chimpanzees on that day had the strange feeling that the chimpanzees quickly understood Dennis had died, even though he had passed away in a separate room, while the group was gathered in the separate indoor enclosure.[80] Dennis was a father figure for all of them, and now, he was dead and gone for good.

Chimpanzees are clearly able to distinguish between death and life. In the wild, females may carry their dead offspring around for hours. However, it's obvious by the way they carry them that they know their babies are no longer alive. It also appears that chimpanzees expect that death can happen, that they are aware of its existence and even that it might occur due to a serious illness. A British researcher, James Anderson, once witnessed the death of an older female chimpanzee in a British safari park. She was seriously ill in her last days, and the members of her group nursed her, tending to and caring for her and apparently also checking her vital signs. Shortly after she died, they stood up and each of them went on with their own activities, as though they immediately knew it was all over.[81]

The fact that animals can mourn, or to be more precise, that animals can display behavior which is difficult for humans to interpret as anything other than mourning, has been documented beyond a doubt. Several unrelated studies have observed chimpanzees in mourning. The chimpanzee researcher Geza Teleki once saw a group of wild chimpanzees gathered around a member of their community who had fallen from a tree, broken its neck and died instantly. They stood around the dead chimpanzee, holding onto and embracing each other with nervous facial expressions. They kept returning to inspect the body, to touch and smell it. One adult female returned alone and sat quietly for a whole hour beside the dead chimpanzee's body.[82] Love is nature's way of getting us to care for one another. Sorrow is the price of love.

Now it was the Kristiansand community's turn to experience loss. It was a quiet, unusual Christmas. The king was dead and the group was without an heir. The female chimpanzees, Sanne, Lotta and Bølla, and their three young males, Julius, Billy and Kjell, were now leaderless.

The Moseid family was mourning its own loss that Christmas. It was the first time that Julius would spend the holiday among his own species. Ane and Siv could hardly believe it. How could they celebrate Christmas without Julius? But their dad explained the importance of being consistent. Julius had lived among humans for almost two years, and now, it was time for him to become fully chimpanzee. They could not allow a chimpanzee to take part in human Christmas festivities. Even the regional newspaper thought it was strange: "Julius to spend Christmas among his own kind" read the large headlines on December 23, 1981.

The next day, the family did their best to keep up their spirits. They tried to forget their little chimpanzee friend for a day, after all he was probably happy at the zoo since he was only an animal and didn't have any idea that it was Christmas.

Then, in the late afternoon on Christmas Eve, around the hour when peace on earth was slated to start and the aroma of pork ribs was filling the living room and the church in Vennesla began ringing in the celebration, Edvard Moseid snuck out. He had an errand to run at the office.

A short while later, the tenderhearted zoo director was in his Volvo on his way back home. He drove along an almost empty E18 highway on the calmest day of the year, with the temperatures at 25 degrees Fahrenheit and a snow flurry whirling on all sides.[83] And seated in the passenger seat, a two-year-old, wildly happy chimpanzee hopped and clambered about. Julius was coming home for Christmas. Moseid couldn't let his girls be sad on this special evening.

Billy Glad called Edvard Moseid to wish him a Merry Christmas and immediately sensed from Moseid's guilty tone of voice that something had happened. "You didn't go get Julius, did you?" a horrified Billy Glad asked.

"Yes, yes I did," Moseid had to admit.[84]

The local newspaper was right: Julius would spend Christmas among his own kind.

Chapter 5

MONKEY BUSINESS

"Those who know the great apes only through
reading or by casual observation of specimens on the stage
or in zoological gardens cannot appreciate either
the intelligence or the emotional traits of the animals."[85]

ROBERT M. YERKES

HUMANS HAVE ALWAYS been fascinated by the capture and display of exotic animals. Historians believe there was a zoo of sorts in Ur, what is now southern Iraq, over 4,300 years ago.[86] And for almost just as long, unusual animals have been collected as rare objects and offered as gifts between powerful rulers. Alexander the Great had 11,000 animals among his collection, William the Conqueror's son, Henry I, initiated a collection of living animals for the royal English crown in the 1100s, and the first chimpanzee likely came to Europe in 1640, imported from Angola and delivered to the Prince of Orange.[87] The royal houses used these animals as props in public displays of power and wealth. The more exotic and rare the animal, the more importance it held as a status symbol. It was a widespread, persistent tradition, one with aspects still visible in modern times. The U.S. president, for example, always brings a dog into the White House, while various celebrities flaunt their ownership of rare animals, such as Michael Jackson with his chimpanzee, Bubbles, or Justin Bieber and his capuchin monkey.

Public zoos weren't established until after the French Revolution, many of them acquiring animals from royal collections. In 1795, a zoo was opened in the Jardin des Plantes in Paris based on the royal collection from Versailles. In 1828, the Zoological Society of London founded a zoo in The Regent's Park with exotic animals previously housed in the royal collection. The London Zoo soon became the model for modern urban zoos that were now springing up all across Europe and North America, such as in Amsterdam in 1838, Berlin in 1844, Copenhagen in 1859 and Central Park in New York in 1862.[88] These zoos were architecturally impressive; they were popular parks for recreation and amusement among the European upper classes, and they presented themselves as institutes of scientific study as opposed to the former royal curio cabinets. Concern for the animals and their needs was a low priority, however, as there was more interest in showing off modern humanity's victory over what was then believed to be wild nature. In the 1920s, the ideas of animal handler Carl Hagenbeck of the Tiergarten Zoo in Hamburg directly influenced a shift toward the modern zoos we know today with naturalistic, three-dimensional facilities mimicking nature, multiple types of species sharing the same space, and canals separating the animals from humans instead of fences and bars.[89] However, it was still more important for it to appear as if the animals were doing well than for them to actually be happy. It was not until Julius's lifetime and the final decades of the 1900s that zoos increasingly became more concerned about the animals' actual welfare and stimulation.

It is often noted that the heyday for modern animal parks rose in parallel with the Industrial Revolution and modern urbanization. In other words, human interest in seeing animals grew as it became less and less common to interact with animals on a daily basis. Because Norway was industrialized much later than many other countries and was largely an agricultural society throughout the 1800s, the country never established a large city zoo for its citizens. When the Kristiansand Zoo was founded, there were two other small Norwegian zoos. But neither could hold a candle to Europe's more expansive zoos.[90] Norwegians preferred seeing exotic animals when traveling abroad or on television. This is why it is not surprising that the NRK episodes about Julius made a strong impression on Norwegian viewers. It was unusual to see live footage of a Norwegian chimpanzee. It just so happened that Julius was also the right animal at the right moment. Mass popularity for zoo animals has shifted over time from the exotic and bizarre to the adorable and cute. A beer-guzzling Russian black bear and Jumbo the Elephant, which both came to the London Zoo in 1865, were typical zoo attractions in the 1800s. Today, newborn animals are the largest draw for visitors. Perhaps the best example is Knut the polar bear, who was born at the Zoologischer Garten in Berlin in 2006. The Internet quickly helped to rocket Knut's status as a global zoo star with the result that attendance at Berlin's zoo increased more than 30 percent in 2007.[91]

Modern zoo-goers no longer wanted to see strange, scary animals but rather those that were sweet and human-like. Even though Edvard Moseid was a passionate animal lover, he was also responsible for a commercial institution with dozens of employees and enormous expenses. He knew Julius had the potential to become a brand name for the zoo. Ten years earlier, the zoo had a similar experience when Judy, a young baboon, was injured after birth and needed rescuing by the zookeepers. Judy slept in a doll's bed located in the zoo offices and was dressed up in doll clothes. Her plight had captivated the press and generated attention for the zoo; however, she was never reintegrated back into her group and eventually became aggressive toward humans. After she scratched one of her keepers and drew blood, the zoo was forced to put her down.[92] Judy was thus an example of both the potential and the danger of Julius's developing story. For the time being, however, Moseid decided to focus on the potential.

THE STRANGE DREAM

Now that Dennis was dead, the zoo was going to have to find a new alpha male to lead the chimpanzee group. All chimpanzee colonies need a leader who can mediate conflict situations and maintain peace and order. They decided to import Champis, a six-year-old male from Borås Zoo in Sweden. It is extremely difficult to import male chimpanzees into existing communities. Chimpanzees have a natural skepticism toward outsiders. While wild females may be able to mate with individuals from other groups, a male chimpanzee could be in mortal danger amongst the wrong crowd. It's possible in captivity to introduce new female chimpanzees, but it is almost impossible to do the same with males without first removing the leader. Because the community's leader was gone, Champis's odds were therefore better than other males who switch colonies. Nonetheless, it was going to be a time-consuming process. Lotta and Sanne had taken over the leadership following Dennis's death. They had been leading for several months and couldn't understand why this Swedish whippersnapper had suddenly arrived with the intention of taking over. In addition, Lotta was physically stronger than Champis and once attacked and threw him into the moat. Champis would have drowned if the keeper had not seen the incident and been able to rescue him.[93] After that, Champis broke down physically and mentally and developed a stress-related rash in the mucous of his mouth, which Billy Glad analyzed and described in a research article published in an American primatology journal.[94] The leaders of the zoo had hoped that the female chimpanzees would accept Champis because he was so young. But their plans had gone awry. They could now see that it was going to take time. Their new strategy was to divide the group, putting Champis in with a only a few chimpanzees at a time until a period when all of them would grow used to him, and they could become a single community unit once again.[95]

This was the first time that the Kristiansand group would have a new leader. But Jane Goodall had observed many such successions within the colony she followed in Gombe. A male is usually eligible to become the alpha male only when he is between twenty and twenty-six years of age, thereafter sinking in hierarchical status after turning thirty. Male chimps are often ranked lower toward the ends of their lives.[96] Physical shape, aggression, ability to form alliances, intelligence and courage are among the primary attributes of an alpha male. Intelligence may trump physical strength; there is no correlation between size and social status. Goodall observed how Mike, a low-ranked chimpanzee in 1963, was able to bluff his way to the top in 1964, not by strength, aggression or courage, but by his use of human artifacts. Mike collected discarded kerosene cans from Goodall's camp and was one of the few chimpanzees daring to take and use these human objects. He banged on them and made loud noises that scared the other chimpanzees, in this way winning the group's respect.[97] Mike's behavior thus proved a wild parallel to the captive Julius's familiarity with handling and using human objects, behavior which also stirred the interest of others in the Kristiansand community. The other chimpanzees often watched, perplexed, as Julius played with the water bowl, driving it around like a car. Some of them even began imitating his strange game.

Compared with chimpanzees in the wild, Champis was too young to be an alpha male. Among the Kristiansand chimpanzees, however, he was the oldest male. Though his caregivers were able to help him win the position, Champis had to fight to keep it and was sometimes forced to act violently in order to earn the others' respect. One of the first times that Champis was released together with the entire group as their alpha male, he attacked poor Kjell and tore his anal mucosa. Julius would also feel the sting of Champis's fury, but up until this point, he had been able to adapt to his new leader. During the winter of 1982, Julius's social standing improved bit by bit. There was less whimpering, complaining and hanging from the door handle out to the human world. He slowly learned the complex social workings of a chimpanzee community and had finally accepted his place at the bottom of the social hierarchy. He and Kjell developed a particularly close relationship. Kjell developed more and more abnormally. He did not grow like the others, his movements were odd and slow and there was always a strange, crestfallen expression across his face. Sanne did not concern herself much with him, but Julius stepped in like a loving big brother. He would often sit for long periods with Kjell on his lap. The fact that Sanne allowed him to sit like this was a sign of sorts that Julius had been accepted as socially valuable. Julius now had a task within the group, he had found a role and thereby a place.[98]

With the arrival of spring, Julius was able to join the others out on Chimp Island. The chimpanzees loved the light and the springtime when they were finally able to go outside again. The island afforded a much larger space to romp and play while the public watched at a good distance from the other side of the moat.

This was new and unknown territory for Julius. He was therefore first brought to the island on his own. In April 1982, the zookeeper Jan Erik Jansen took Julius out to the island for the first time. He was allowed to clamber around on the heather and trees and to experience for himself that the area was not dangerous.[99] He was taken back again several times and Ane and Siv Moseid were once again tasked with playing with Julius so that he would feel safe in these new surroundings. But once again, the process had to be broken off abruptly.

On May 19, 1982, Julius hurt his finger during play and was taken to the Glad family home for an operation. He was anesthetized, sewn up and returned to his cage while still asleep. But his sleep was unusually heavy during the evening and it was apparent from his screams that he was having nightmares. No one wanted to leave him until he woke up. Grete Svendsen offered to take an overnight shift with him, but she had to return to work at 7:00 the next morning. So Billy and Reidun Glad decided to take him back home to Bliksheia and let him sleep in the bathroom there. Reidun went and got the mattress, the same one from the first night when Julius had stayed with them three years before. She lay down beside Julius for one more night. He slept through the night, with Reidun dozing off and waking throughout. At 6:45 a.m., Julius woke up. He opened his eyes, looked directly at Reidun, and shut them again. Then he opened them again, looked directly at Reidun, shook his head as though waking himself up for real, before shutting his eyes again and squeezing them tight. Chimpanzees, like humans, dream when they sleep. Their rapid eye movements and increased brain activity verify this. The way that Billy Glad interpreted this episode was that it seemed Julius believed he had only dreamt that he was at home with Reidun and that he was trying to help himself fall back asleep in order to finish his unusually lovely dream. Maybe he had often dreamt about something similar back in his cage in the zoo? But when Julius opened his eyes for a third time, he became excited and was wide awake and happy, realizing that his dream was in fact a reality: he was at home with Mom.[100]

A CONTROVERSY AND CROWD-PLEASER

Julius stayed with the Glad family for a week. Billy Glad monitored the wound and checked to make sure it was healing properly. At the end of the week, Julius was sent back to his post at the zoo. The summer season was approaching and interest in Julius as the park's main attraction was increasing. Norwegian children sent him fan mail. A five-year-old boy mailed a small down blanket to the zoo so Julius wouldn't freeze at night. The public was expecting a tame chimpanzee on their visits and the zoo couldn't resist the mounting pressure. Throughout the summer, Julius was taken out of the Tropical House and Chimp Island to roam the park and encounter guests. Åse Gunn Mosvold was among the zookeepers who regularly took Julius on these excursions. She would first isolate him from the other chimpanzees in the enclosure with branches before entering and taking him out. She would then carry him around the zoo as though he was a small child. They climbed trees, picked berries, turned over rocks to wonder at all the insects creeping underneath and played simple games like hide-and-seek and tag.[101] Adoration of Julius only intensified after zoo visitors returned home with stories of their own close encounters with Julius. He regularly stole ice cream and cake from park visitors. He was just unpredictable and mischievous enough to perpetuate the myth of a rascally and hotshot human chimpanzee.

The media interest in Julius was a constant and overwhelming storm. Edvard Moseid worked himself to the bone. He lived in and for his job and had done so since 1967, often working seven days a week and suffering a variety of injuries from confrontations with animals of all sorts. The explosion of media attention focusing on Julius had thrust Moseid and his family to fame nationwide. None of them liked the attention. It was an unhealthy situation and Moseid grew ill from all the pressure, undergoing two serious stomach operations during this period. Yet Julius's fame only grew.

In the spring of 1983, the NRK TV series about Julius was broadcast again for the fifth time, if one counts both the children's television and school broadcasts. Trygve Bj. Klingsheim and photographer Arild Jakobsen were wrapping up the final details for a soon-to-be published children's book about Julius, which had already received a flurry of interest from foreign publishers at the international children's book fair in Bologna. "In the making of this book, Trygve Bj. Klingsheim held the pen," wrote the newspaper VG, as though the journalist's work had consisted of little more than capturing Julius's own version of his life thus far.[102]

Whenever individual zoo animals become renowned, it is nearly always the case that their characters are anthropomorphized and discussed in public as though they were speaking creatures. It was as if two versions of Julius now existed and had parted ways, each living out their own separate lives. On one side was Julius the public brand and zoo ambassador, a regular recipient of fan mail and the subject of newspaper headlines, whose face adorned posters in countless childhood bedrooms across Norway. On the other side was Julius the misfit, a confused creature who did not know where he truly belonged, who feared retribution from his community's alpha male, and whose only friend was his developmentally disabled younger brother, Kjell.

The children's book by Klingsheim and Jakobsen was hyped up before it was even published. However, the coverage of its launch in May of 1983 created an equal amount of buzz. Julius attended the launch, and "signed" copies for some of the luckiest guests with a marker on page 2. The first edition print run of 10,000 copies soon proved to be too low. Before the year was out, 50,000 copies had been sold. At the book launch, someone remarked that Julius was the only chimpanzee specimen in the world who had lived among humans and been successfully reintegrated back into a chimpanzee community.[103] This was, of course, untrue, but the newspapers were uncritical in repeating anything that might render Julius even more unique and interesting to their readers.

Other "serious" Norwegian authors grew jealous of the book's enormous success. When the outspoken critic and author, Odd Eidem, returned home to Norway the following year from his house in Provence, he didn't mince words, stating that he felt he had returned from Provence to the province. Norwegian literature was stale, he claimed in a large newspaper article in *Aftenposten*. The only good book that year, he said, had been authored by Julius the chimpanzee.[104] Not recognizing the irony in his statement, the author Sissel Lange-Nielsen felt provoked by Eidem's quip and responded that she could easily list ten good works of Norwegian fiction from 1983 that wouldn't even include Julius's book, which she had not yet read.[105] Eidem's intention, of course, was not to cast a pall over Norwegian authors. He was rather criticizing the booksellers who prioritized the sensation of Julius over newly written literature: "When, to the exasperation of my colleagues, I proclaim the primate Julius to be the bestselling author of the year, of 53,000 copies, Sissel Lange-Nielsen would do well to look up the word 'irony' in the dictionary," he explained in a new article.[106] The sales figures for Julius's book were a symptom of a culture in crisis, Eidem believed. It was a sign of cultural degradation that people could be so enthralled with something as idiotic as a chimpanzee.

Poor Julius was both a controversy and a crowd-pleaser at the same time. Norwegian authors discussed him with disdain among *Aftenposten's* cultural pages, while his photograph regularly graced the pages of several Norwegian tabloids. The zoo began to experience an enormous influx of visitors. The total visitor count went from 110,000 in 1982 to 360,000 in 1983. The increase wasn't only due to Julius. In May of 1983, the zoo had also opened a new amusement park built for roughly $3.5 million USD, with an amphitheater, a racetrack, trampolines and a 1,700-foot-long toboggan course. The new development was part of an international trend. Traditional zoos across Europe were struggling with attendance and making ends meet and many of them had decided to adapt to modern times by transforming into combination animal and amusement parks. To mark the inaugural celebration for the new amusement park area, a newly-penned folk ballad about Julius by musician Terje Formoe was performed for the first time. A crowd of 1,400 people gathered in the amphitheater when Formoe sang his song along with a full band, and before the last verse was over, Edvard Moseid surprised the audience by appearing on stage with Julius in his arms. The melody was simple and catchy like mainstream pop music. Formoe was of the opinion that only grandparents, and not children, enjoy listening to traditional children's songs. Children, he believed, prefer pop music. And Formoe obviously had a good ear for children's tastes because the song quickly became an enormous hit. Children of all ages sang along to the lines: "Here comes Julius who all want to see / Swinging from the top of a tree." "I like the song but I'm not particularly proud of the lyrics," Terje Formoe confessed many years later.[107]

In addition to the book and song, a new type of Julius soft drink was unveiled followed up with a Julius LP album that was produced in 1983. Julius was no longer only the zoo's primary attraction but now represented all of southern Norway. "He was our best tourism director," said the actual tourism director of Kristiansand, Helge Sundsvik.[108] The zoo was overwhelmed with calls from birthday party organizers, festivals, film companies and advertisement agencies all hoping to rent or borrow the chimp. Edvard Moseid tried to keep a balanced perspective. He could still allow groups of visiting children to come into close contact with Julius, but it was difficult to make the children understand that they had to be careful. Julius was a familiar figure from their children's television programs. He was almost a person and it was hard for the children to understand what Edvard was saying when he explained to them, in his mild southern Norwegian accent, that it could be dangerous to touch Julius. Sometimes when the children ate ice cream or drank soda pop while watching Julius, he would suddenly grab their sweets. This behavior got a laugh from the children, but it was not especially safe. Moseid made up his mind that the summer of 1983 was to be the last summer for children to interact directly with Julius at the zoo. "Julius has started to bite and hit. I'm glad. It shows that he is a chimpanzee," said Moseid.[109] Similarly, he decided that from this point on, his daughters Ane and Siv Moseid would only be able to visit Julius from the other side of the moat. They would no longer be permitted to touch him. Now Julius had to sit at the edge of the water calling across toward them while Ane and Siv sat at the fence calling back. "I really miss Julius. I think about him every night," said Ane.[110]

When it came to PR, the topic of Julius was caught between a rock and a hard place. The more he behaved like a real chimpanzee, and the more successfully he became integrated into his own community, the more it increased the disappointment of his public. Many visitors had trouble distinguishing him from the other chimpanzees on Chimp Island or in the Tropical House. Why can't he wear diapers like in the pictures? some would ask. It was only when he was behaving brashly, lobbing rocks at Moseid and random visitors and playing his role as Julius the Joker that he lived up to their expectations.

From early on, Moseid had sensed the enthusiasm that this adorable chimpanzee might arouse. But in his wildest dreams he had never imagined the tsunami of attention that now flooded the zoo. Moseid was completely blindsided. The public interest was certainly a symptom of the commercialization of entertainment that swept the country during the so-called "yuppy-wave" of the 1980s in Norway. At the same time, the fate of Julius also represented a timeless fascination. The dividing line between primate and human has always been intriguing. The topic has been handled in fiction again and again.[111] In films and showbiz, chimpanzees have successfully been trained to act like humans. Chimpanzees have been used in circuses and carnivals; some of them have even had their own TV shows on American channels while others have been regular film stars. Cheeta, the chimpanzee featured in the Tarzan films from the 1930s and 1940s is possibly the world's most well-known chimpanzee with his own "autobiography" that was published in multiple languages.[112] Stemming from the same macabre preoccupation with the blurry lines between primate and human is the obsession with humans who resemble chimpanzees. For several hundreds of years, such people have been able to make a living as objects of curiosity among various freak shows. The most notorious example was the so-called Ape Woman, Julia Pastrana, born in Mexico in 1834 with an appearance so closely resembling a chimpanzee that a doctor had to verify she was a human. She immediately became a freak show sensation but died at the young age of twenty-six in Moscow. Death, however, did not terminate her career. Her body was mummified and she continued to go on tour as a carnival attraction, eventually landing in the hands of the Norwegian carnival founder, Haakon Lund. Pastrana's cadaver joined Lund's curio cabinet at his amusement park and was displayed on Norwegian and international tours until as late as 1971, 111 years after her death. Her body was later stolen and then rediscovered in a landfill in Groruddalen in Oslo before being sent to the Forensic Institute at the Gaustad Hospital in Oslo.[113] Just eight years after Pastrana's body had been publicly displayed for the last time, Julius was born, a very animated and accessible creature who was half chimpanzee, half human.

Chapter 6

A FUGITIVE CROSSES HIS TRACKS

"One of the most striking aspects of chimpanzee society is the relative autonomy enjoyed by every individual after the age of about nine years. [...] This freedom in choice of companions, travel route, activity, and so on, plays an important role in reducing stress, particularly for males."[114]

JANE GOODALL

T IS THE oldest cliché of biographies. At the precise moment that the biographical subject finally gets their big breakthrough with work, offers and media attention, their private life also reaches its darkest point. Julius was no exception. In March 1984, NRK broadcast a new episode about Julius on children's television, an epilogue of sorts to the three previous episodes that had summed up his unusual story and captured the great transformation in his life, namely that he had become a much sought-after and beloved VIP chimpanzee. The Julius book continued to sell, surpassing 75,000 copies in 1984 in Norway, and plans were underway to publish translations in Denmark, Sweden, Finland and Iceland that fall. At the same time, Julius's life among the other chimpanzees was proving more challenging for the main character. The level of conflicts increased. Champis would often behave brutally toward Julius and both got into frequent skirmishes in which they would shove, hit and bite each other.

· Opinion is varied about why the integration process, which had long been successful, took sudden a turn for the worse. Some believe that Julius suffered from his frequent extractions out of the community to be with humans and that this amplified those aspects of him that made him an oddity among the other chimpanzees, in turn complicating his life as a zoo chimp. Others theorize that it was due to Julius's approaching adolescent phase, claiming that it was only now that the effects of having been rejected by his mother were starting to play out. Whatever the reason, other events occurred in the chimpanzee community, which destabilized the group as a whole and further pushed Julius into an even more precarious position. On March 9, 1984, Bølla gave birth to a stillborn chimpanzee. And a short time after her baby's death, she also died. Then, on the night of May 1, 1984, Lotta bore a male baby that was given the name Bastian.[115] Because of Bastian, Lotta's older son Billy was largely left to fend for himself. Up until that point, Billy's mother had protected him through thick and thin, but now a new individual had arrived and usurped his comfortable position. Suddenly Billy was without protection in the community—much like Julius. This instability in turn placed a greater demand on Champis, who was often strict and heavy-handed with the younger chimpanzees. In order to keep the peace in the group, the keepers isolated Champis from the rest of the chimpanzees for long stretches of time.

In an attempt to improve the mood of the group and to provide the younger chimps free time away from Champis, an additional outdoor island was constructed for the 1985 season. It was dubbed Julius Island. Billy, Kjell and Julius were given free rein of the island on summer days. Here they were allowed to romp and frolic without fearing any sort of retribution from Champis, and from here it was also easier for visitors to catch a glimpse of Julius, an obligatory highlight on their zoo schedule.[116]

Although Billy and Julius were similar in age, it was never hard for the public to figure out who was who. Julius interacted much more frequently with the visitors than Billy, often sitting at the water's edge and gesturing with his arms toward the people. He threw moss and rocks to catch their attention. Or he pooped into his right hand and flung his feces toward the public. Because of such behavior, he was a more interesting attraction than the other chimpanzees, but at times he could be unpredictable and unsavory. He had become something of an abnormal zoo chimpanzee, which in fact was quite normal for chimpanzees separated early from their mothers. An Austrian-Dutch research team followed the outcomes for many of the young chimpanzees that were captured in the wild between 1950 and 1980 and taken to European, Japanese and American zoos and laboratories. Their research showed that these chimpanzees had incurred clear emotional scars, regardless of whether they had been kept in sterile research labs or integrated into large chimpanzee colonies in modern zoos. Those individuals who had been removed from their mothers when little participated less often in grooming than other chimpanzees, even after they had lived with the group for several decades.[117] Other research results have arrived at the same conclusions: Steve Ross at the Lincoln Park Zoo has been involved in over thirty transfers of chimpanzees living among humans to zoos or research centers. He followed the individuals after they have been successfully reintegrated into their groups and was surprised at the amount of time following integration that the chimpanzees continued to struggle with deviant behavioral tendencies. Even many decades after being returned from their lives among humans, these chimpanzees still stand out from the rest of the individuals in their group. They display noticeably peculiar behavioral patterns, they give and receive much less grooming than the other chimpanzees, they are unconventional and remain outliers in their groups.[118] In other words, Julius was reacting normally by developing into an abnormal zoo chimpanzee.

BABYSITTING FOR BASTIAN

On September 9, 1985, Lotta also died. She was only sixteen years old at her death and weighed only slightly more than 90 pounds. The autopsy report concluded with a series of diagnoses from bronchitis and lung inflammation to liver disease and emphysema.[119] Thus, in a short time span, both Billy and the one-year-old Bastian had become motherless. Billy was almost self-sufficient and would be able to survive without his mother, but Bastian was much too small to fend for himself. He required milk and care and safekeeping from all of the threats that might take place in a chimpanzee community.

The zookeepers tried enticing Sanne into taking on a motherly role with Bastian. And at first it appeared their tactic might work, but one day she suddenly bit Bastian forcefully, flung him away from her and signaled clearly that she wanted nothing more to do with him.

After this incident, the keepers tried to interest Julius and Billy in assuming responsibility in much the same way that older siblings often care for younger ones in the wild. Julius had proven how caring he could be when Kjell was little, and he now assumed a similar role toward Bastian, at least whenever there were humans present. As soon as Julius was left alone with Bastian, he began shoving and biting the baby. When the zookeepers would return, often running because of Bastian's screams and yelps, Julius would once again switch into his caring and compassionate mode, tenderly watching over the baby chimpanzee. It was strange behavior but the pattern repeated itself over and over again. Eventually, it became apparent to the zookeepers that Julius was playing a conscious game for human attention. He used Bastian as a pawn to gain recognition from his caretakers.[120] Just as other prominent figures, Julius had become addicted to attention. Human attention may even have trumped his empathy for the helpless little chimpanzee.

There were now four young male chimpanzees in the community but none of them was completely normal, Billy Glad concluded in an internal note about the status of the chimpanzee group. Bastian was motherless and an outcast. Kjell was physically impaired, possibly also mentally. Billy fluctuated more than the others. At times he could be characterized as a disruptive element and the type of chimpanzee that the park should get rid of, but at other times he was perceived as "the nice guy," the kind of chimp that the park should value. Julius was clearly marked by his foreign upbringing. He was "always a bit of an outsider to the others," wrote Billy Glad. "Now and then rowdy, but lately he has mostly been the object of aggression from Champis."[121]

Besides the four young male chimpanzees, there were only two adult chimps left following the deaths of Bølla and Lotta: Sanne and Champis. Thus, Champis was a leader without challengers for the small chimpanzee group consisting of only one female and four young males. Even so, much time and effort was required on the part of the keepers to maintain the peace in the community. But the staff had many other animals to care for as well, and there were limits to how much time and resources they were able to put into this one species. In order to discuss what might be done, the zoo formed a chimpanzee working group in 1985. The group met for the first time bright and early at 7:30 a.m. on October 29. Edvard Moseid opened the meeting with an introduction in which he floated the idea of whether or not the zoo should even have chimpanzees at all. The matter was discussed for two hours. Grete Svendsen was of the opinion that "the situation with the chimpanzees is hopeless."[122] In the end, they all agreed to keep trying and to prioritize and professionalize the care for the chimpanzees. The specific plan of action was to remove Bastian from the community, to place Champis on the powerful psychiatric medication, Haldol, and to set in motion certain measures that would activate the group, such as spreading honey and raisins across the mountain in the indoor pen.[123] Bastian was first isolated in his own cage where the zookeeper Hilde Gro

Hummervoll would be able to care for him. When she had gained his trust after several months, she was able to act as his foster mother, similar to the models of Moseid and Glad. The weekly tabloids latched onto the story and added the embellishment that Julius was to assume responsibility for Bastian once he returned to the group. It was easy to project that Julius could remember and understand what it meant to be an outcast in his community. "Perhaps something touches Julius's primate heart when he looks at this motherless little creature," *Aftenposten* speculated.[124] In the public narrative about Julius, this would be a lovely turn of events that newspapers and tabloids could sink their teeth into. But in reality, the reintegration of Bastian would prove to be impossible.

ON THE LOOSE

Sanne, the mother of both Julius and Kjell, gave birth to another son on January 29, 1987. He was called Mardon. Zookeepers generally hope for female chimpanzees who are more easily adaptable to the hierarchy as adults and who are also able to bear more chimpanzees. Mardon was the fifth male chimpanzee to be born in a row in Kristiansand.

Only three days after his birth, Sanne died.[125] In a relatively short interval, Sanne, Bølla and Lotta had all died. All of the animals that had lived through the Tropical House fire of 1978 were now gone. Champis was now also without any harem. Julius missed his mother even though he had never experienced much motherly love from her.

There was no one left in the community who could take responsibility for Mardon. By this point there was also little hope of reintegrating Bastian. It would be easier for him to start over again among a new community. Mardon and Bastian were thus turned over together to Öland Zoo in Sweden. In return, the zoo received a four-and-a-half-year-old female chimpanzee who they hoped might be a good partner for Julius.[126] She arrived in Kristiansand on February 9, 1987 and was first placed into quarantine. The PR idea was to introduce her as a girlfriend of sorts for Julius—even if she was too young to be a mother. A wild female chimpanzee usually gets pregnant for the first time around the ages of twelve to fourteen. However, in captivity it is possible for pregnancy to occur many years earlier. The idea was that she and Julius might live separated from the rest of the group and start their own family.

At this point, Julius could use a fresh start. In close quarters with Champis, his days were anything but easy. Champis scared and punished him on a daily basis; he was often so brutish toward Julius that the zookeepers were forced to intervene. Julius was therefore frequently isolated or kept for hours with only Billy as a companion. But even that combination had the potential to go south, with Billy and Julius sometimes coming to blows so violently that the zookeepers would have to separate them by spraying them with water hoses.

Thursday, May 30, 1987 was a particularly bad day. Champis had been extremely hard on Julius, and so he had withdrawn to a hiding place just beneath the rafters of the Tropical House ceiling. Here Julius could sit for hours alone without fear of reprisal from the alpha male. And so he sat and thought. Just as the human, the chimpanzee is an animal that is able to contemplate the solution to a previously unknown problem. This was demonstrated by the German psychologist

Wolfgang Köhler, one of the pioneers of chimpanzee research in the early twentieth century. Through laboratory experiments, Köhler was able to show that chimpanzees could think their way to the solution of a problem they had never previously considered. As an example, he would hang fruit up on the ceiling or place it out of their reach outside their cage, and after a small period of thought, the chimpanzees would realize that they could reach the fruit by stacking objects on top of each other and climbing up onto the stack. Or that they could fit one bamboo stick into another until they had a tool long enough to reach the fruit outside of their cage. Köhler was not primarily interested in whether they were able to achieve the tasks but rather how they went about discovering the solutions. His point was to show that the chimpanzees did not solve the problems by trial and error but through contemplation and a sudden flash of insight. This phenomenon, this sudden insight into the solution of a problem, is still referred to as "a Köhler-moment" in chimpanzee literature.[127]

Now it was Julius's turn to have his own "Köhler-moment." As he sat up beneath the rafters, hiding from Champis, he discovered something that he had never noticed before. He saw a potential escape route via a few of the ceiling beams. A bit later, while he was down on the ground among the other chimpanzees, he suddenly jerked in realization. A feeling of unease spread through the community as Julius began to run amok, whooping loudly before grabbing onto one of the climbing ropes and climbing all the way up to the ceiling and out along the rafter beams. One of these beams had an electric pulse designed to prevent such an escape. It was possible to see the shock given to Julius's body as he passed it, but he was so determined to get out that he continued on. He climbed on the rafters over the moat and dropped down on the visitors' side in the Tropical House. From there, he darted straight toward the exit, pushed open the door and went out into the park. A few visitors who had been inside the Tropical House were shocked witnesses to the situation, among them the freelance photographer Knut Uppstad, who snapped pictures of Julius as he was climbing, and dashed after him out into the zoo.[128]

A seven-and-a-half-year-old chimpanzee was on the loose. The arms of an adult male chimpanzee are five times stronger than those of an athletic adult man. Because a chimpanzee attacks with all four hands, it is practically impossible for a human to defend him or herself. A chimpanzee's bite is also powerful. In fights, chimpanzees often crush one another's bones with their teeth.[129]

That same day, seventy children with cancer had traveled on a chartered flight from Tromsø, in the far northern region of Norway, to visit Julius, among other attractions. But upon entering the Tropical House, they found that he was gone. Indeed, at that moment, Julius was sprinting down toward the administrative area, across the parking lot and into the café. Many of the visitors merely stood by smiling and guffawing about Julius the Joker, who was once again out among humans. The café was promptly evacuated, but Julius ran into the bathroom. In doing so, he had entered a trap. It was easy to shut him inside. They locked the door, and with that, had him under control. The zoo staff got a delivery van and the keeper Åse Gunn Mosvold decided to be the one to go in with Julius. She took a deep breath and uttered a quiet prayer. She knew that her own fear was the greatest danger. Any sign of fear would give Julius the psychological upper hand. She was able to control her fear, however, and walked calmly into the bathroom, took Julius by the hand and led him outside into the waiting van. Julius was driven straight back to the sleeping quarters where he was allowed to calm down for the rest of the day, before being released back into the common enclosure with the other chimpanzees.[130]

Upon his return to the group, new confrontations with Champis swiftly broke out. Five days later, his keepers discovered severe bite marks on Julius's body. It was necessary for Billy Glad to examine and treat the wounds. To medically examine a seven-year-old chimpanzee without anesthesia is usually impossible, but in this case, Glad was able to treat Julius almost like a human. It turned out that the bite marks had been created with canine teeth. This left no doubt about exactly whose canine teeth were in question. "Champis's attitude is clearly aimed at the total destruction of Julius," Glad concluded.[131]

Violence is an important part of everyday life for chimpanzees, and in the wild, they have been known to kill one another during internal conflicts. However, chimpanzees usually avoid letting their conflicts become too serious. Aggression is so central to chimpanzees that they have had to develop a range of techniques in order to keep clashes from escalating too easily or too often into serious brutality. When two male chimpanzees provoke one another, there is almost always a buildup phase before they come to blows, thereby allowing a window of time during which it is possible for a third party to act and calm down the rivals. During this phase, the opposing chimpanzees prefer to stand and sway with their upper torsos, bristling and making noises with increasing volume. By contrast, there is no warning when two female chimpanzees clash.[132] The canine teeth of female chimpanzees are not as long as those of males. A brawl between two females is therefore not as dangerous as between two males—a fact which may be the evolutionary explanation for why nature has equipped male chimpanzees with more warnings and therefore more opportunities to avoid a real fight. Male chimpanzees in a community are always dependent on one another regardless of internal rivalries. In hunting and in battles between external enemies, against other colonies and when defending their own territory, the chimps are dependent on one another's physical prowess. Those male chimpanzees that destroy one another in internal struggles will not be able to protect their own community and will thus not be able to pass on their genes. This is why there is a clear code for the majority of internal fights between males; they usually use their sharp canine teeth only on fingers and feet, but seldom on a rival's head or shoulder. They measure strength within a common framework almost like two athletes. It might even seem as though the human practice of competitive sports is nothing more than a continuation of our evolutionary background. Perhaps sports developed as regulated competitions, just as a rivalry in a primate community could determine who was the strongest and thus had the right to lead the group— and the right to propagate his genes—without anyone getting hurt, as hurting one another would destroy their common goal of protecting the group against their external rivals.

For this reason, reconciliation is paramount for chimpanzees. Two chimpanzees that have recently fought will seek peaceful bodily contact with one another surprisingly quickly following a fight. They are attracted to each other like magnets, wrote Frans de Waal. In less than a minute after a fight has ended, the dueling parties might seek out and kiss each other and initiate a mutual grooming session, nursing and tending to their coats and skin and any wounds. Frans de Waal has data to show that no other chimpanzees spend as much time on mutual grooming as two male chimpanzees do during the period in which they are in conflict with one another.[133] This rapid reconciliation following a huge brawl does not happen without some misgivings and defensiveness. The two rivals will often mope around waiting for the other one to take the initiative, bringing to mind a kind of code of honor.[134]

Chimpanzees are dual-natured animals and have both aggressive and reconciliatory sides. Julius and Champis were better at aggression than at reconciliation. Neither of them would initiate reconciliation, and Julius refused to be subservient. Nor were there any female chimpanzees able to intervene to dampen a conflict between the two males. The Kristiansand community was an artificially composed group with a limited territory. Levels of aggression are often higher among chimpanzees in captivity than in the wild because they have less space to hide or withdraw when trouble is brewing, and also because they have more spare time to kill. Julius had been captured and locked in with an aggressive and physically superior leader. He had no one to help him, and he had very little space to hide. His only way out was to escape. He had managed it once before. He would try it again.

"JULIUS IS IN LOVE"

The Swedish female chimpanzee, who was intended as a companion for Julius, had finally concluded her quarantine period. While in quarantine, she had been close enough to Julius for him to smell and hear her, but now when they were first brought together in the same enclosure, Julius treated her callously and was so rough with her that the zookeepers were forced to intervene several times.[135] Things were not exactly off to a good start, yet the zoo still launched a targeted PR campaign in the summer of 1987 to draw attention to Julius's new "girlfriend." Readers of Norwegian issues of Donald Duck comics were invited to submit names for the new female chimpanzee, even though she had already been given a Swedish name while living at the other zoo. The zoo received over 20,000 submissions for names, if one is to believe the zoo's chief of entertainment, Terje Formoe.[136] Most of the suggestions were something akin to Julia or Juliane, but the zookeepers suspected that these names would not work well when calling out for her. They tested out their hypothesis, just to be certain, and Julius reacted to all of the options that were similar to his own. Therefore at the end of July they reached a decision to call the female chimpanzee Josefine.

Josefine was not sexually mature and neither she nor Julius appeared to have any interest in one another, yet the media celebrated the whole thing as a romantic event. "Fortunately, everything went as hoped. She lay down and accepted her subservience. They were sweethearts. It was time for love and affection," was Edvard Moseid's eager interpretation.[137] This kind of "engagement" story fit perfectly into the public narrative of Julius's life, which was presented to match a human's life as closely as possible from the origins of his sweet childhood via a challenging adolescence and up until the moment when he would now establish himself as an adult. A love story and the idea of the two lovebirds, Julius and Josefine, was a natural continuation of this income-generating myth.

Julius was a superstar and the tabloids covered his love life with as much intrigue and devotion as they granted to other superstars. "Julius is in love," declared the headline of *Norsk Ukeblad*. Their competitor, *Hjemmet*, expounded in their headline: "Julius is in love, deeply and innerly."[138] In the chimpanzee world, however, falling in love is not really a thing. Nor do chimps have romantic relationships. Chimpanzees are not monogamous. An evolutionary biologist has only to quickly glance at the testicles of a male chimp to prove it. A male weighing under 110 pounds has testicles weighing over 3.5 ounces, which is twice the size of an adult human's and more than double the size of a gorilla's testicles. The reason has to do with their sexual habits. While humans are generally monogamous and gorilla leaders have an exclusive monopoly on sexual access to females in their groups, chimpanzees are more promiscuous. The alpha male does have a certain amount of control and first sexual claim but oftentimes, whenever a female is in heat, several males have a go and the fight over which of them is allowed to pass along their genetic material is closely linked to which of them is able to produce the most sperm. This sexual situation has favored chimpanzees with larger testicles than those of humans or gorillas, for whom this particular trait has not been as evolutionarily critical.[139]

Nonetheless, many of the power struggles among chimpanzees have to do with sex. Although they are promiscuous, their sexual etiquette doesn't allow for free-for-alls. Access to sex and the monopolization of female chimpanzees is key to many of the conflicts between males. And access to sex is an obvious source of pleasure for both genders. Males can forget to eat for many days at a time while females are in heat, and Frans de Waal has noted the way in which the Arnhem community males would wake up in the morning in their sleeping pens with eager looks in their eyes on those days when they knew they are going to be let out among female chimpanzees in heat.[140]

There is no natural birthing season for chimpanzees and thus mating can take place all year long. A regular menstruation cycle for a female chimpanzee is thirty-six days, and the days during which she is fertile are apparent from the swelling of her genitalia. It is during this period that female chimpanzees are most active. However, mating activities are not limited only to this schedule, particularly so in the case of captive chimpanzees. Female chimpanzees hold much more power when they are in heat, with research showing that they have longer grooming sessions when they are in heat than otherwise, and that they have a higher success rate at begging food from males that have gotten ahold of something to eat.[141] There is also a game that takes place among the males for the right to sex. Male chimpanzees in Arnhem groom one another nine times longer than usual when one of the females is in heat, and it appears that this may be a payment system of sorts in which a lower-ranked male is able to earn the right to couple with a female by grooming a higher-ranked male.[142]

Female chimpanzees, however, sometimes have their own sexual preferences that fly in the face of the community's hierarchy, choosing to mate only with certain select males. In fact, two female chimpanzees in Arnhem had such strong preferences that appeared to parallel a more human system of falling in love with only one particular individual. These females did mate with other male chimpanzees, but whenever they themselves initiated mating, their overtures were aimed at only one chosen male. Furthermore, before mating with the male of their choice, they would always perform their own "sex dance" as the researchers call it, in which they danced and displayed themselves for their partner. This dance was reserved exclusively for the preferred male.[143]

An advanced social game is required before chimpanzees have intercourse. The act itself, on the other hand, is short lived. To be precise, chimpanzees finish within seven seconds.[144] Jane Goodall's meticulous researchers in the Gombe in Tanzania, who count and record anything that can be counted, have reached the conclusion that male chimpanzees release their sperm on average after 8.8 thrusts of the pelvis.[145]

Once again, Julius got to have everything for free, as for the time being, Julius, Josefine and Billy were to live together apart from the others. As long as he was able to crack the code, Julius was granted unlimited sexual access to a female chimpanzee without the need to rival an alpha male and without the need to earn his reward with long periods of grooming. During the same period, two additional adult females, called Dixi and Bini, were imported from Munich to be paired with Champis so that he would have other things on his mind besides his dislike of Julius. Julius, however, seemed erotically uninterested in Josefine. Although she was much too immature, the zoo-keepers had at least hoped that Julius would show curiosity and initiative when faced with such a golden opportunity. Moseid was worried that Julius's upbringing among humans may have interfered with his natural sexual education that usually begins very early on for chimpanzees. After a while, Moseid began to wonder whether Julius might be homosexual. During the early stages of Julius's puberty, he had often tried out his impulses on his shorter younger brother, Kjell. Moseid contacted other zoos to see whether they had any experience with homosexual chimpanzees.[146] Homosexuality is wide-spread across nature. Its existence has been proven among over 1,500 species, with a frequency varying from 40 percent among rose-breasted cockatoos to only a few percent among humans. In addition, there are some species in which every sexually mature individual is bisexual. Moseid didn't know what to think. He didn't take his thoughts public but decided to wait and see. Perhaps Josefine was simply too young?

The media hype around Julius's romance was good for business. The zoo sold 7,000 plush Julius toys every season as well as the same number of Julius-themed T-shirts. Also available for purchase were Julius backpacks, Julius sheets, dozens of different Julius posters, Julius puzzles and even a Julius game created by the producer Damm. By the summer of 1987, the book by Klingsheim and Jakobsen had sold 85,000 copies in Norway and had now been translated into seven languages, including German, English and Hebrew. The Julius TV series had been adapted and shown in several countries, and in Finland, it was broadcast on all three of the country's channels.[147] The zoo's marketing and entertainment chief, Terje

Formoe, thought up the idea of issuing a pop music award that he would call the Julius Prize. Norwegian pop artists were invited to compete for the annual Julius worth $2,000 USD.[148] But what Norwegian pop music had to do with an identity-befuddled zoo chimp, and why the prize should bear his name, and why exactly a zoo should suddenly become a destination for music-lovers, was not exactly clear. Of course, it all boiled down to the personal network of the zoo's marketing and entertainment chief, Terje Formoe—himself a well-known Norwegian singer—and to the zoo's constant efforts to keep the Julius brand fresh. However, this PR stunt was a sign that the Julius theme was being stretched very thin. The two dueling identities of Julius were growing further and further apart; the fictional Julius was handing out pop prizes while the animal Julius was being placed more and more frequently into isolation.

The weekly newspapers didn't notice that the chimpanzee team had abandoned their strategy of isolating Julius, Josefine and Billy away from the rest of the group. Instead, the three had been returned back into the common enclosure with the other chimpanzees, though with the new rule that Julius and Champis were never to be present at the same time. The two male chimpanzees would alternate spending time with the community. In practice, this meant that Julius was held in isolation for an entire day, while Champis was together with the group. On the next day, the opposite would occur.

The Kristiansand chimpanzee group was now made up of Billy, Kjell and Josefine, the two new females Dixi and Bini, and Champis or Julius, depending on the day. It didn't take long for the keepers to see that both Champis and Julius were

frustrated by the new schedule. They were angry at being isolated and would remain angry on the days when they rejoined
the group.[149] It was not possible for Julius to be with Josefine
on the days when he was in exile. The idea of a kindling relationship between Julius and Josefine turned to ash as rapidly
and easily as it had ignited. Josefine would become a member
of the larger group, available to pair with whomever she preferred when she was ready.

"IT WAS A LITTLE SCARY"

Although he was no longer in contact with Champis, Julius
was still unable to settle down into the community. He had
a wanderlust that distinguished him from the other chimpanzees. On September 18, 1988, on one of the days when
Julius was mixed in with the group, he once again managed
to escape from Chimp Island and venture out into the zoo.
Using a long stick, he jumped up to the roof and bolted from
there. He made a beeline toward one of the zoo cafés, apparently with the aim of finding food, but when he passed the
popular log slide that had been opened in 1986, he seemed to
have another idea. He climbed up to the loading dock of the
ride and splashed water on the people standing there. Few
of the guests realized how dangerous the situation was but
the internal alarm had long since been sounded, and Edvard
Moseid, who in that moment had been driving around in the
park in a rental car, turned and headed straight toward the
log slide. Julius didn't recognize the car but Moseid got out
and called his name. At first, Julius walked calmly toward
Moseid but then changed his mind and sprinted back toward

the crowd and freedom. Moseid hurried up to the closest kiosk and asked for a few cartons of chocolate milk. He went back to the car and held the cartons up in the air while calling for Julius. The craving for sugar proved to be stronger than his craving for liberty, and Julius walked over to Moseid and offered his hand in exchange for chocolate milk. Moseid gave him the milk, took his hand and ushered Julius calmly into the car.[150]

Julius managed to make a mess of the car during the short ride back to the Tropical House. He sat in the back seat drinking chocolate milk through a straw. Edvard Moseid received an extra bill after he returned the car, though he publicly downplayed the incident and dismissed the idea that it was dangerous for a nine-year-old male chimpanzee to be running around amongst hapless children.

Julius's escape attempts were perhaps not so unusual. Some zoo animals make hourly escape attempts. Kristiansand Zoo has had its share of incidents too. On one snowy winter night in 1974, all thirty camels got out via a snowpack over their fence and made a caravan along the E18 highway. A kangaroo had escaped through a wall and was run over and killed by a car. Two female sea lions, Veronica and Roxanne, once snuck through the fence near their bathing area and escaped out of the zoo. One of them was recaptured at a riding arena on the other side of the European highway, the other managed to get further and hung around in the southern forests and various waterways all the way back to the ocean. She was observed five weeks later on a reef before vanishing for good. Two years after a storm off the coast of Uruguay had washed her ashore and a villager had brought her to a zoological garden, she had arrived back at the same ocean on the opposite side of the world.[151]

Other animals have tried and succeeded at short outbreaks. But Julius's escape attempts were different. While the other animals were escaping to the wild, back to their natural habitats, Julius would set a straight course toward humans. He ran to kiosks and cafés and people and fun.

It was hard to know how best to secure the facility, since Julius was obviously more interested in finding ways out than in being together with the other chimpanzees. His escapes were an expression of a new and more difficult phase in his life. The newspapers interpreted his actions as puberty troubles, but for chimpanzees, this phase is much more complex than the physical process of becoming sexually mature. In the wild, male chimpanzees have a long and arduous youth. They reach sexual maturity when they are eight years old, but are only socially mature when they are around fifteen. During this transitional stage, they must distance themselves from the babies and females in their group, though they are not yet accepted among the adult male chimpanzees. Wild, young chimpanzees in this phase often leave for days to be alone or go to their mothers for comfort when the adult males aren't looking. Neither of these alternatives was an option for Julius. As a captive chimpanzee, there was nowhere he could choose to be alone. And he did not have a mother to whom he could turn. As if that wasn't enough, he was a being split between two identities, his life as a zoo chimpanzee on the one hand, and on the other, his life among humans.

On Tuesday, May 23, 1989, Julius managed to escape once again. Somehow, late in the afternoon just before closing time, he was able to cross the moat and get out. There were still children roaming about the zoo. Chimpanzees are predators and there have been instances in the wild when chimpanzees have captured and eaten human babies. In the administrative building at the entrance of the zoo where the ticket office was located and where employees had their office spaces, twenty-year-old Kristin Fausa was alone at work. The other staff members had left for the day, though Edvard Moseid and Jan Erik Jansen were still in the park when a message was suddenly sent over the intercom that Julius had escaped. In the seconds that followed, Fausa received a message that she should immediately lock the door to the office building because Julius was heading in that direction. The keys required to lock the door from the inside, however, were inside a key cabinet and before Fausa was able to reach the cabinet, she saw Julius outside. He had been in the parking lot beyond the gates of the zoo, but he turned around and began running back into the zoo in the direction of the administrative office. He was visibly angry and excited and banged aggressively on the hoods of a few remaining parked cars as he sprinted toward the office's glass door. Fausa had not had the chance to lock the door and now stood somewhat doubtfully holding onto the doorknob so he wouldn't be able to open it. Julius walked straight to the door and looked in rage through the glass at Kristin Fausa. He sauntered down the small staircase and Fausa thought for a moment that he had given up and decided to go elsewhere, but in fact he had only backed up in order to get enough speed. He began to run and throw himself at the glass, shattering the windowpane into shards that rained down on Fausa before continuing into the office. Fausa stood in shock beside the smashed door while Julius darted around in the open office space. Julius had spent a lot of time in this office when he was younger and had probably expected to meet Moseid and others from the old days. Going from desk to desk, he pulled down papers and books and binders, throwing and smashing things as though in a planned act of vandalism until he realized that none of his old acquaintances were there, so he dashed outside again straight past Fausa and into the café in the adjacent building. Some of the park guests were at tables finishing up their meals, and families with children soon ran screaming from the building. The whole scene was reminiscent of a bad horror flick. People ran for the parking lot and Julius chased after them out of the café, but then Moseid and Jansen showed up. Walking calmly but decisively over to Julius, they each took one of his arms, as though he was an arrested criminal, and led him back to the Tropical House. As they passed the office, Julius made eye contact with Fausa and sent her what she interpreted to be a threatening, cautionary look. Just wait, Julius seemed to be saying with his eyes.[152]

It was an impressive capture by Moseid and Jansen. Julius still had enough respect for and connection to each of them. Perhaps they were even the people he had been seeking during the whole time of his escape. But for the zoo visitors and Kristin Fausa, the experience was traumatic. Julius had put dents in several of the cars on his rampage through the parking lot, and the guests had to fill out damage reports before leaving so the zoo could assume responsibility and pay for repairs.

The newspaper *Fædrelandsvennen* was tipped off about the ordeal and wrote an article about it. "It was a little scary," Fausa admitted to the newspaper. A few other papers printed smaller articles about the story, but Moseid wanted to put a lid on it. And clamp it shut. None of the newspapers mentioned the damaged vehicles or Julius's mad flight through the offices. Mention of the topic then became more curious than scandalous. Moseid was annoyed that Fausa had publicly admitted to being scared. He called her into his office to remind her that all communications with the media should be directed through him. He himself downplayed the incident on the Norwegian News Agency, NTB. He promised to tighten up security measures, but maintained that "Julius is not a danger on the loose."[153]

The zoo never discovered how exactly Julius had managed this particular escape. Perhaps he leapt across the moat some way or another. Chimpanzees are usually afraid of water since, unlike cats and dogs, they cannot swim instinctively and will drown if they fall in. But although there are zoo chimpanzees who have been taught to swim and who have eventually learned to swim breaststroke in deep water, it was extremely unlikely that Julius had taught himself how to swim.[154]

The consolation in the midst of this otherwise turbulent phase in Julius's life was that he and Josefine were getting along much better and could therefore be released together on Julius Island on the days when it was Julius's turn to be separated from the rest of the group. What's more, they had finally cracked the sexual code. On the zoo's twenty-fifth anniversary in 1989, Crown Prince Harald came for a visit to see Julius, among other reasons. Julius was given a large helping of bananas and, according to the plan, would thereafter perform a few monkey tricks for his royal guest. But Julius had other plans. He was horny and very busy trying to mate with

Josefine.[155] Moseid had worried whether or not Julius would be able to figure out his sexuality due to his upbringing among humans. But nature took over. Julius had figured it out. (In 8.8 thrusts of the pelvis.) Crown Prince Harald wandered discretely off in another direction.

Chapter 7

CRIME AND PUNISHMENT

*"This isn't permanent. But for the time being
we have no idea what to do. Julius is too smart."*[156]

EDVARD MOSEID

THE 1980S WERE over. *Aftenposten* regional newspaper asked its readers to select the southern Norwegian of the decade and, of course, they selected Julius.[157] The eighties had been his decade. But now, though only eleven years old, he was on the downswing. As long as he still couldn't find his place in the community and father his own offspring, Julius's life would continue to be incomplete and disharmonious. The zoo held out hope that he would become a father. In the same way that new births help to solidify a monarch's institution, the zoo hoped that a successful birth of a Julius–fathered baby chimp could help to buffer up his brand. Josefine was still young and she had yet to get pregnant. But Julius didn't give up. When he was together with the larger group, he had been observed several times mating with Bini, one of the two adult females that had been imported from Munich three years earlier. In the winter of 1990, it became clear that Bini was pregnant and though Josefine had been the publicly lauded girlfriend of Julius, the newspapers began to titter about whether Julius might be the father of Bini's baby. In March, Bini was quarantined until the birth. Following the birth, the zoo planned to take a blood test to determine fatherhood. The baby arrived on May 9, 1990, the first female baby chimpanzee to be born in Kristiansand. The tiny creature was called Bitten, but her blood test pointed to Champis as the father, and so the new chapter in Julius's adventure would have to wait.[158] By the next fall, Josefine was finally pregnant and there was media speculation over whether Julius would soon become a father. Julius was suddenly plunged back into his monogamous relationship with Josefine in the public sphere. "For three years he has lived in partnership with the 8-year-old Swedish Josefine. The zoo hopes the relationship will result in a growing family," wrote *Aftenposten*.[159] It was as though Julius was held above journalistic standards. Journalists wrote whatever story seemed most convenient at the time.

While Josefine's pregnancy progressed and the zoo awaited her baby's arrival, other factors were threatening the zoo's entire existence. On May 22, 1991, around 2:30 p.m., a dangerous fire broke out near the zoo. The summer had been dry and the underbrush easily caught fire and began to spread rapidly. There were strong winds that day, optimal conditions for fanning fires and terrible working conditions for firefighters. During this summer season, the zoo had planned to open its largest attraction to date, namely a full-scale life-size version of author and illustrator Thorbjørn Egner's Cardamom

Town. The crown jewel of Cardamom Town was a tower in which the town's fictional weather forecaster character, Tobias, would reside. But now it was Edvard Moseid darting up the tower steps to gaze down on the blaze. If the fire came any closer and the flames entered the zoo, he would be forced to refer to his so-called death-list, a list of all the dangerous animals that he would quickly have to kill before the zoo could start thinking about evacuation. Julius and the other chimpanzees were high up on this list. "I can barely finish the thought. But in the worst case, we will have to let the safest animals fend for themselves and kill the most dangerous ones," said Moseid.[160] All of the animals were taken indoors and given a helping of particularly good food. Julius and the other chimpanzees were put into escape-proof cages and fed as though it was a birthday feast.[161]

The fire departments from three different municipalities were all called in, as well as the civil defense and the emergency service of the Red Cross, volunteer scouts and a special helicopter that dumped 2,853 quarts of water over the fire throughout the night. But they were unable to control the fire, and no one could say whether or when the flames might reach the zoo. On the NRK daily review at 7:30 p.m., a report stated that the zoo was not in danger, but four hours later on the evening news, the situation had turned for the worse. "Fire officials believed the zoo to be safe this afternoon, however this evening the fire has blazed up again," they reported. Shocked firefighters watched in horror as the flames hopped from treetop to treetop. At 9 p.m., it was possible for the first time to smell smoke within the zoo's confines.[162] "We will stay all night," Billy Glad said when he realized the wind had once again shifted direction toward the park. It was an all-nighter for the zoo employees while the firemen battled the flames. The fire department decided preemptively that they would prioritize the parts of the zoo where animals were still alive and allow the dead areas, such as the fully completed but not-yet-initiated Cardamom Town to burn down.[163]

In the end, it was the wind that decided the course of the fire. The flames were northeast of the zoo, encompassing 247 acres and sending the frightened wild forest animals from their habitats. Several elk ran across the E18 highway, and one of them was hit by a car. Throughout the evening, the flames were only a few hundred meters (or a few thousand feet) away from the zoo. Julius and the other chimpanzees, who in nature, live deep in forested areas and thus instinctively know to avoid fires, must have sensed the smoke that entered the park. Military personnel arrived to assist the firefighters. The forest between the fire and the zoo was doused with water to stop the blaze from spreading in that direction. But in the middle of the night, the wind seemed to change its mind. Julius's life would be spared. The fire altered its course and never reached the zoo. Late into the night the fire department was able to report that they had control of the blaze, though putting it out entirely would require a few more days.[164]

When the zoo finally returned to normal, Josefine was the news story that received the most attention. She was not yet even nine years old, which was relatively young for a chimpanzee mother, and for this reason she was closely monitored for the remaining weeks until the birth. Veterinarian Gunn Holen Robstad wanted Josefine to be alone for the birth. The best scenario would be if Josefine could be kept indoors during the day and give birth to the infant inside while the other chimpanzees were out on the island. The zookeepers thought she appeared quick and lively on June 24, 1991, and so they let her out together with the other chimpanzees even with a possibly imminent labor.[165] And, as fate would have it, her contractions began once Josefine was outside. She climbed a tree to give birth as wild chimpanzees instinctively do. It was a fast birth, the infant came out within a few minutes but Josefine wasn't fast enough to grab hold of him. He fell down from the tree and straight into the moat where he drowned instantly. Shocked visitors witnessed the drama. The zookeepers fished the baby out of the water and tried giving him first aid but without success.[166]

King Harald and Queen Sonja were planning to visit the zoo three days later during their national tour as the newly crowned royal couple. The zoo had hoped they would be able to greet a newborn chimpanzee with a famous father. The last time the couple had visited, they had witnessed an attempt at producing just such offspring. This time, they encountered a chimpanzee community in mourning. "The king greets a sad Julius," *VG* wrote in its headline.[167]

JULIUS ON THE ATTACK

It is doubtful whether Julius was truly sad. He had neither understanding nor expectations of what it meant to be a father. It was different for Josefine. Chimpanzee mothers usually mourn their stillborn babies. Sometimes, zoo personnel cannot get hold of dead chimp infants for hours because the sorrowing mothers hold so tightly on to their young.

But even if Julius was not particularly moved by the drowning death of his baby, there was still a palpable sense of unrest in the group. Åse Sundbø was on the first week of her new job as an animal keeper in September of 1991, and she noticed that something unpleasant was brewing. The chimpanzees were ill tempered and uncooperative; they threw their food as soon as she had served it, and Julius and Champis were frustrated at being held in isolation every other day. She had to make absolutely certain that the right doors were closed so that they wouldn't accidentally come into contact with each other.

Suddenly she heard that Julius had been seen up on the roof of the Tropical House. He had managed to escape yet again. A guest had noticed him and asked Edvard Moseid's father, Endre, who just happened to be passing at that moment, whether it was okay for a chimpanzee to be swinging about on the rafters. Endre Moseid immediately realized the gravity of the situation and signaled to the administration to sound the escape alarm. Jan Erik Jansen arrived to help Åse Sundbø recapture Julius. She had never experienced anything so frightening in her whole life, though Jansen, who had been in similar situations before, was impressively cool and collected. When Julius began walking straight at Sundbø, she got so scared that she sprinted into the Bird House and locked the door. Jansen fetched some bananas and treats and threw them into the Tropical House enclosure to coax Julius down. The strategy worked. Food trumped freedom. Julius climbed down by himself, as one of the other keepers quickly shut the opened roof panel. Few of the visitors realized what was going on and nothing had been damaged, but the experience was nonetheless frightening. Once again, no one knew which escape route Julius had chosen this time around, or how he had been able to climb to the roof.[168]

It's hard to keep chimpanzees penned up. They are extremely good climbers, can hop incredibly far distances, are smart and cunning and can learn from trial and error. In fact, several of the Kristiansand chimpanzees might have been able to escape if they only had a similarly intense desire to do so, like Julius. But the others didn't have much incentive to take off. They were served their food; they were kept safe and happy in captivity and knew little about the potential dangers in the vast world on the other side of the moat. Julius, on the other hand, had been out there hundreds of times. The most likely explanation is that he wanted to get out to be among people. All of the attention he had received when he was little had made him dependent on more complex social stimuli than what he got from his monotonous life in captivity. In fact, he cared more about humans than about other chimpanzees. There were people who existed out in the world that he appeared to miss deeply. And there were people he seemed to hate.

The zoo's garbage collectors belonged to this latter category. Julius despised the loud tumult of the garbage cans being emptied just outside his sleeping area. Noise is a signal of power in the chimpanzee world, and perhaps Julius perceived the noise as a challenge. Oddvar Ivarson had just started his job as a garbage collector at the zoo in June 1992, but had already learned of Julius's dislike of him. On the evening of his second day of work, he stood with his back to the chimpanzee pen lifting bags of garbage when Julius suddenly threw himself against the glass behind him, as though to grab or to scare him. Ivarson thought it was funny and responded by banging on the unbreakable glass with his fist. Julius was not amused.[169]

The next evening, on Sunday, June 7, 1992 around 7:00 p.m., Ivarson was once again out on his daily rounds. He was driving a truck around the park with a colleague. His thirteen-year-old son rode on the stepping board at the rear of the truck. What they didn't know yet was that Julius had once again escaped. This time he had discreetly snuck out of the Tropical House and hidden behind a souvenir kiosk. He was waiting for the daily garbage collection. He had been able to escape from Chimp Island unobserved, and now he sat in ambush. He was going to get them. As the truck passed the souvenir kiosk, Julius burst out of hiding. It was the colleague that first noticed him. "Julius is coming!" he screamed. Ivarson saw Julius in the rearview mirror and, fearing that he would grab ahold of his colleague or his son, he sped up but Julius ignored the two people on the stepping board and ran up alongside the truck's cab. Ivarson hoped feebly that Julius was out on some other errand, but Julius knew precisely what he was after. The truck window was open and Julius leapt onto the vehicle, grabbed hold of the side mirror and swung in through the window. Ivarson stopped the truck and tried holding Julius off with his left hand but Julius bit the watch off his arm and entered the cab, falling into Ivarson's lap between his body and the steering wheel. Ivarson hit Julius as hard as he could, striking his ears multiple times but Julius didn't appear to notice. He was stronger and grabbed hold of Ivarson's fist, bending his index finger up and trying to bite it off. He bit down, but the angle was off, and he ended up giving Ivarson a scar from the tip of his index finger down to his palm. Blood spurted out into the cab. Ivarson's colleague had climbed up onto the roof of the truck and was trying to help him through the window. His son ran up and pulled open the cab door on the passenger side, but was shocked to see his father's blood as he fought the adult chimpanzee and ran screaming down to the duck pond below. Ivarson screamed as loudly as he could, from fear or pain, and this powerful scream may have saved his life. Julius jumped out of the car through the window, saw two security guards and began to run in their direction. The only thing for the guards to do was to turn and run and they barely managed to stay ahead of Julius.[170] By that point, the alarm had been sounded and Jan Erik Jansen once more began the chase. Julius was still trusting enough of Jansen that he was able to put an end to the difficult situation with little trouble and guide Julius safely back to his cage.

Oddvar Ivarson was driven directly to the West Agder Hospital. The tendons in his finger were severed, and he feared amputation and membership in Edvard and Julius's exclusive club of those living without a finger after a brutal meeting with a chimpanzee. However, the doctors were able to save his finger by grafting skin from his arm to patch his palm. The wound developed complications and inflammation from having been bitten by the teeth of a chimpanzee. Ivarson was hospitalized for two weeks and never regained full mobility of his finger's fine motor skills. It was fortunately only his left hand, he comforted himself.[171]

When Ivarson had recovered, he returned to his job at the zoo. Edvard Moseid paid for his missed time but begged Ivarson not to go public with the story. A few sources had witnessed what had happened. None of them was able to get Ivarson to talk. Moseid once again suppressed the issue, but this time he took it very seriously internally. Ivarson had agreed to keep the incident under wraps under the condition that Julius would never, ever be able to escape again.

CHIMPANZEE MORALS

This was the fifth time Julius had gotten loose, and it was by far the most dangerous. The zoo had to do something. The employees mulled over what might have motivated Julius. It was a brutal and seemingly meaningless action on Julius's part, but was it immoral? Can chimpanzees have morals? They can, in any case, follow rules; this has been proven beyond a doubt. They can learn to follow human-created rules in zoos, and they can also understand that there are consequences to break-ing these rules.[172] But in the wild, they also follow their own chimpanzee rules without any human interference. Among them the rule of reciprocity, for example, that the chimpan-zee who helps another may expect help in return. Since they live in a group and have exceptional memories, reciprocity has developed as an effective mechanism for companionship. Chimpanzees know that they will *receive* when they *give* and they are able to conduct advanced transactions such as shar-ing a bite from a hunt in exchange for grooming the hunter. A pleasure-for-food exchange.[173]

But in order to be able to talk about morality, or a type of animal precursor to what we humans call morality, we must go one level deeper than rule-regulated behavior and reci-procity. We must at least be able to talk about empathy and whether chimpanzees are able to understand that their fellow creatures may be in pain, whether they can understand their own role in causing the pain, and whether they may be able to express some kind of remorse. All of these criteria are in fact very clearly present among chimpanzees: chimpanzees help each other to treat and rinse wounds and injuries. If an individual in a wild community is hurt and wounded, the others may care for them, wait on them and slow down their pace. In addition, a chimpanzee who injures another during a fight may attempt to alleviate his rival's pain during the reconciliation phase. Chimpanzees who have caused harm to each other know exactly where to find the wound. It is obvious that they understand the consequences of the injuries they have inflicted, they remember where they have struck the other chimpanzee, and they realize it causes pain. They also know what needs to be done in order to alleviate the pain caused by the injury.[174]

In addition, their empathy can extend beyond their own kind. There are many examples of chimpanzees helping wounded birds or other animals. The chimpanzee, Lucy, who lived for twelve years with the human Temerlin couple, made obvious attempts to comfort her human "parents" if they were in pain. If they had the flu and were puking into the toilet, Lucy would often run after them to the bathroom and stand behind stroking their backs as they vomited.[175] Chimpanzees may even take enormous risks by saving and helping individuals to whom they are not related. Biologists can discuss *why* this happens but not *whether* it does. Reciprocity may of course be able to explain some of it. The chimpanzee who saves another in need may hope for help in return if ever he or she lands in trouble. But there are many examples of wild chimpanzees adopting motherless chimp babies, a service so costly that they will never truly be repaid. And it isn't only the female chimpanzees that do this. In a research project along the Ivory Coast, a total of ten male chimpanzees over a period of thirty years were observed adopting motherless chimpanzee babies who were not related to them.[176]

All of these factors indicate that it may be possible to imagine a simple kind of morality between chimpanzees. There are also factors suggesting that they are able to feel shame and remorse about what they have done. The German zoo director, Bernhard Grzimek, was once seriously wounded by a chimpanzee, however in the aftermath, he experienced that the chimpanzee displayed a rare and intense concern for him and desire to tend to and treat his injury.[177] During the days when Kristiansand zookeepers still went inside the chimpanzee enclosure, one employee noticed that Dennis had become very upset. He threw her up against the wall and struck her hard. She escaped with her life, but the next time the keeper encountered Dennis it was clear he wanted to beg pardon. He crept toward her subserviently, took her hands and gently nibbled on her fingers like a dog.[178] When the chimpanzee Lucy became relatively advanced in sign language, she was the first chimpanzee to put to words this type of remorse or shame. She revealed her ability to lie, or at least, to attempt to deceive. While living with the Temerlin couple, she accidentally pooped on the floor. The sign language expert, Roger Fouts, asked her whose feces it was.

"What's that?" he asked.

"Lucy not know," she replied.

"You do know. What's that?" Fouts repeated.

"Dirty, dirty," Lucy answered.

"Whose dirty, dirty?" asked Fouts.

"Sue's," Lucy answered, trying to blame one of the other ASL researchers who worked with her.

"It is not Sue's. Whose is it?" Fouts insisted.

"Roger's," Lucy tried again.

But when he once again refused, she gave up:

"Lucy dirty, dirty. Sorry Lucy."[179]

This dialogue is interesting on several levels. It shows a kind of consciousness about truth and lies, as well as the ability or desire to hide the truth. It also seems to display a sort of sensitivity to shame. Lucy did not fear any form of retribution, such as concrete physical punishment for the accident as this was neither the first nor last time something of a similar nature occurred in the living room. Nonetheless, she appears to be ashamed about what she did.

An even more amazing reaction was that of the chimpanzee Washoe—the pioneering subject of the great sign language wave of experiments—when one of her keepers gave birth to a stillborn baby. The keeper was away from work for a lengthy period during her pregnancy, stillbirth and time of mourning. Upon her return, Washoe acted apathetic and distant as she always did when one of her keepers was gone for a long time. The keeper decided to tell Washoe what had happened and showed her the ASL-sign for "my baby died." Washoe, who had lost two babies herself, gave her a bewildered stare and then replied with the ASL-sign for "cry." Following this, she gently placed a hand on the keeper's face and drew a line with her finger from her eye down her cheek like a tear.[180]

"SING SING"

It is impossible, of course, to know what Julius truly thought about his handling of Oddvar Ivarson. But it is very likely that he was able to understand his role in causing a human pain and that he was also able to take pleasure in what he had done, as well as to perhaps regret it in some way. In any case, he was soon going to have a lot of time to think it over. A lengthy punishment loomed for preventative—if not moral or legal—reasons. As an employer and public institution, the zoo was responsible for the safety of their staff and guests. Thus, over the following days, Julius was banished into his own isolated pen inside the Tropical House, away from the eyes of the public and others. A crisis meeting was called at the park. Safety measures surrounding the zoo's chimpanzee enclosure were already more strictly enforced than regulations required, so it was unclear how Julius had managed to escape five times in six years. The staff believed it had something to do with the skills Julius had picked up during his time among humans, resulting in a chimpanzee who was much too clever for the system. There were serious discussions about putting Julius down, according to *VG*. Not a chance, Edvard Moseid contradicted when the news station NRK questioned him on such reports.[181]

In the end, the park decided that it was best for Julius to remain in isolation, while they hastily constructed what Moseid somewhat rosily called a very own apartment for Julius and Josefine. The finished "apartment" proved to be nothing more than a 325-square-foot green cage with a little red spring rider inside. It looked like a birdcage apart from the fact that the chimpanzees could retreat to a small indoor cage for sleeping. "Fate better than death," *VG* concluded laconically.[182] But the solution was only temporary. Julius couldn't spend the rest of his life in a cage. Moseid was ashamed about the decision. Internally, the cage was referred to as "Sing Sing," after the famous New York prison along the Hudson River.

The first time Julius was let into the cage, he ran around as though checking for escape routes. Some plaster had come off on one section of the brick wall, and Julius quickly went to investigate, jumping against the wall to see whether it might crumble. After that, he tried to dig beneath the cage with his hands, as though believing it might be possible to tunnel under the fencing. The conclusions of his research seemed to irritate him. After a half hour he began throwing stones at the cage while howling loudly.

Zoo visitors who were now able to view the famous Julius in his new surroundings often expressed pity for the chimpanzee. "This is not permanent. But for now, we honestly don't know what to do. Julius is too smart," Moseid would explain.[183] Julius was Norway's most popular animal. He was the southern Norwegian of the decade. He was supposed to be the zoo's main attraction. But he had somehow ended up as a dysfunctional and dangerous, caged chimpanzee.

Garbage collector Oddvar Ivarson was among the few who were happy that Julius now spent his days in an escape-proof cage. It had been a traumatic experience for him. His son had had frequent nightmares about Julius. Once, while walking around the zoo, Ivarson was suddenly curious whether or not Julius would still be able to recognize him. He decided to walk past his cage, keeping his distance behind a large crowd of people who stood looking at Julius. But Julius picked up on him at once. He became clearly very irritated, dashing wildly around in the cage and picking up small stones that he lobbed with all his might through the bars toward Ivarson.[184]

So much for chimpanzees' ability to regret their behavior.

Chapter 8

FOUR WEDDINGS
AND A FUNERAL

*"The management should have come to realize
that the male chimpanzee Julius is a frustrated and wayward
being whose existence has been utterly destroyed."*[185]

GUNVALD OPSTAD

THERE IS LITTLE truth to the oft-repeated claim that only healthy and happy zoo animals are able to bear young. The caged life of Julius and Josefine was sad. It was a temporary solution to a crisis situation and not exactly a model for exemplary animal handling, but at least the two of them had each other. They did whatever they could to keep busy whenever they were together. And soon Josefine was pregnant.

Nonetheless, it was a long winter for Julius and Josefine. Their keepers tried their utmost to stimulate the two chimpanzees within the confines of their dismal little cage, but during winter hours, employees went home at 3:30 p.m. Staff members would feel pinpricks of guilt at the thought of the two animals spending sixteen long, dark hours alone until humans returned to the zoo.[186] But they managed to get through the winter and on May 15, 1993, Josefine bore a little son and Julius became a father. The last time, everything had gone wrong during the birth, but the zoo had learned from the loss. They were not certain how Josefine would handle her role as a mother, and so they waited to announce the birth to the public. The mother and child were confined and kept under watchful eyes for three weeks before the zoo finally shared the news. It was only on June 4, 1993, coincidentally one day after the Kristiansand Zoo became listed on the stock market, that the *Dagsrevyen* news program was allowed to broadcast the first photo of the young chimpanzee named Julius Junior. Several newspapers quickly picked up the story, though not with the same measure of gusto that Julius had received at his own birth.[187] Josefine and the baby were still in confinement, but if things went well, the baby was to become an important attraction for the zoo at the end of its 1993 summer season.

A sociology professor at the University of Oslo, Stein Bråten, who was working on a book about basic communication and social interaction among humans from birth to old age requested to research how these things functioned in the chimpanzee world. He was granted permission for fieldwork in which he would observe, note and describe Josefine's behavior toward Julius Junior. Professor Bråten lay in watch in the bushes and was thus able to see how surprisingly resourceful Josefine was when, on one occasion, Julius Junior suddenly stopped breathing. Junior was unable to cough or cry, but his mother soon figured out what was wrong. Bending over her baby, she placed her large mouth over his and sucked out a blade of grass that he had put into his mouth. She pulled the blade out and held it up in triumph to show to her keepers.[188] Still, Josefine was not a particularly good mother for Junior. She sometimes treated him the same way that Sanne had treated Julius. "She [...] holds the baby out away from her, and sometimes even upside down. The baby looks like he is starting to grow weaker," Bråten observed twenty-five days after the birth.[189]

Julius was still living behind his caged bars while the zoo worked on building an escape-proof indoor Ape Jungle. The plan—or the dream—was that this new enclosure would allow Julius to live safely and harmoniously with the rest of the chimp community. The zoo now had a total of eleven chimpanzees, including Julius, who would all join him in the new Ape Jungle: Josefine and Junior, Kjell and Billy, the alpha male Champis and the two adult females Dixi and Bini. Bitten, Bini's small female baby, had died in her first year as so many chimpanzees do. Dixi had borne three males: Jesper, five years old, Leo, one year old, and her new baby, Tobias. The reason that she was able to bear Tobias only one year after Leo's birth was because Dixi had rejected and bitten Leo. Leo had been removed from the community and was living at home with Grete Svendsen while the administration searched for another zoo to take him.

Seven of these eleven chimpanzees had been born in Kristiansand, and all eleven could look forward to the opening of the zoo's new indoor Ape Jungle slated for the summer of 1994—a brand-new 14,000-square-foot enclosure with the price tag of roughly $1.6 million USD. The layout of the new quarters had been intended to allow the chimpanzees to live in surroundings reminiscent of their natural habitat, while simultaneously giving the public the chance to see them up close in the winter and on cold and wet summer days. In addition, the possibility for escape would be completely eliminated.[190] A doorway and a bridge enabled the eleven chimpanzees to go to and from their indoor Ape Jungle out to the old outdoor Chimp Island. For the time being, however, the door and island were shut off while the zoo worked on updates and escape-proofing the island as well.

The Norwegian pop star and rainforest advocate, Morten Harket, came to open the new addition on June 24, 1994. Harket and Julius were the two biggest stars of the 1980s in Norway, both of them had posters gracing the walls of countless Norwegian children and both were on the wane in 1994. Morten brought along his wife, Camilla, and their one-year-old daughter, Tomine. The entire family got to meet Leo, the one-year-old chimpanzee, who was carried around by Grete Svendsen. Also in attendance was Ane Moseid, who was all grown up by now and had become a mother herself, and so Edvard was able to walk around with his own one-year-old grandchild in his arms. The meeting was a gaggle of one-year-olds, and the focus quickly turned onto these young beings and their future living conditions. The entire enclosure was presented as an environmental initiative, and this new Ape Jungle as a modern expression of a fresh way of thinking about zoos. During the 1980s and '90s, the majority of zoos had begun to shift their images. While the earliest zoos of the 1800s saw themselves as scientific institutions with a mandate to inform the public, modern zoos more and more often perceived their role as conservationists of species in an escalating environmental crisis. The responsibility of zoos was now to care for and ensure viable populations of species that were threatened in the wild. Of course, the fact remained that zoos were still primarily commercial institutions, but modern zoo visitors were not particularly interested in paying entrance fees to any park where the animals appeared to be suffering. New metaphors arose likening zoos to modern Noah's Arks. This new role was formally established in 1993 with the "World Zoo Conservation Strategy," in which the Kristiansand Zoo naturally took part.[191] If the zoo still had a mandate to inform the public, it was now focused on raising awareness of the Earth's condition and no longer so much on demonstrating humankind's dominion over the wild. "An animal enclosure such as this can serve to show people how a natural environment functions and how vulnerable it is. Those with raised consciousness will learn a lot here," said Morten Harket.[192]

The new Ape Jungle addition was meant to shuffle the zoo into a new era. Edvard Moseid had been at the helm since its inception, but his future with the zoo was increasingly uncertain. His health was poor; he had survived both a heart attack and a stroke and had separated from Marit. On top of that, he was in a legal battle with the zoo's marketing and entertainment chief, Terje Formoe, about the rights to the fictional figure, Captain Sabertooth, who had earned the zoo a pretty penny. It was perhaps time to end this chapter. For the time being, Moseid satisfied himself by rearranging the leadership team and asking the board of directors for permission to go on a longer convalescence trip to Venezuela. With as little luggage as possible, a bible and a Catholic prayer book, Moseid went off into the jungle with the local native people.[193] It was a kind of reverse-Julius pilgrimage. Julius was, after all, a jungle animal who had spent his entire life among humans in a tiny social democratic country just below the North Pole. Edvard was a Norwegian gardener and zoo director who was now leaving civilization behind to venture deep inside the Venezuelan jungle. They were now living each other's lives. Many of the director's employees feared for their boss and saw the expedition as a kind of camouflaged suicide mission.[194] But Edvard returned a few months later, brimming with new energy and new project ideas.

"THE BRIDE HAS LANDED"

For a short period, the whole chimpanzee community lived together in the new Ape Jungle enclosure. But the notion that Julius would simply glide into his new role among the group in the impressive enclosure was short lived. Champis was never going to accept Julius as a member of the group. Julius was defiant and ambitious, and Champis quickly viewed him as a potential rival. The zookeepers tried to keep Champis out of the enclosure for a few hours each day to allow Julius to be with the other chimpanzees. But whenever Champis returned, conflict, rivalry and fighting soon broke out.[195] Once again, Julius and Champis were forced to spend alternating days with the group. As long as it was summertime and warm, this solution was not too difficult. One of them could be outside on the island with the rest of the chimpanzees, while the other had to be inside the enormous enclosure by himself. But when winter came, the isolated chimpanzee would have to sit alone in an indoor cage all day long.[196] It was enough to drive one crazy.

Project Julius was back to square one; he was still an outsider in the group. It was painful to realize that Julius might have to live for twenty to thirty more years under these special conditions and isolation.

As if that weren't enough, Josefine had lost interest in Julius Junior. She did not feed him enough and set him down to be alone for hours at a time or else handed him off to Julius, who would then sit perplexed with his son in his lap, gazing up as though questioning his keepers.[197] The zookeepers had to remove Junior from the community at times to feed him. There were limits as to how many young chimpanzees they could take out in this way, but before they were able to figure out a solution to Junior's problem, he died on March 17, 1995, from pneumonia.[198] The incident received no public attention. It had been apparent that raising Junior into a strong, healthy chimpanzee was going to be a challenge, but the zookeepers were nonetheless distressed about just how difficult it was to bring any sense of normalcy into Julius's life. He seemed unable to gain access to the community, and he was unable to father healthy offspring.

The zoo was also in a crisis. 1995 was an annus horribilis, a terrible year, with the number of visitors falling by 50,000 and a deficit of roughly $2.4 million USD. Terje Formoe resigned and took his fight over Captain Sabertooth to court. Many people in the leadership were forced to step down, but Moseid had returned from Venezuela with renewed vigor. He had regained his old mettle and wasn't about to quit in a crisis. He remained on as director and came up with a strategic plan to return the zoo to its roots. People shouldn't be drawn to southern Norway for pirate-themed rides and a log slide. They should come for the animals; this is where the zoo should return its focus. And was there any animal more valuable to the zoo than Julius?

"It's time to pump some life back into Julius," said Moseid to the new zoo chief, Arne Magne Robstad.[199] Moseid's plan was to form a new chimpanzee group around Julius, to establish a new community with Julius as its alpha male. He hoped to build a new enclosure for this group next to the Ape Jungle, a grotto that would be called the Julius Grotto. He planned to import a female chimpanzee from a foreign zoo with whom Julius would hopefully mate and start a family. The zoo couldn't afford this new venture, and the board of directors could not promise to cover more than a few of the costs, but sponsors started lining up to support the chimpanzee star, and zoo staff offered to work voluntarily to build the new enclosure. Construction kicked off on February 12, 1996. The plan was for it to open as early as May 5.[200]

Julius would thus have his own escape-proof indoor and outdoor enclosure. The indoor enclosure would be 1,075 square feet and feature a towering structure where Julius and his new family could climb among artificial rock formations and even a waterfall. The zoo veterinarian, Gunn Holen Robstad, traveled to zoos in Sweden, Denmark and Germany in search of a female who was strong and healthy and seemed to be safe and confident enough to stand up to the unpredictable Julius. In the Copenhagen Zoological Garden, she found Miff. Miff was beautiful, had a good coat and appeared calm and balanced, according to Robstad. She had been born on August 29, 1987, which meant that she was not yet nine years old and had only recently grown to sexual maturity. In comments to the

newspaper *Fædrelandsvennen,* zoo chief Arne Magne Robstad
said he could not rule out that Miff had never "messed around
with any guys before" but, he believed, it "couldn't possibly
have been all that many."[201]

Miff was scheduled to fly from Copenhagen to Kristiansand on April 23, 1996. Arne Magne Robstad and his wife,
Gunn Holen, traveled to accompany her. It was a long and
unusual day for Miff. Born in the zoo in Copenhagen where
the only chimpanzee enclosure was indoors, she had never set
foot outside in the fresh air. Now she was not only going to fly
for the first time but would also eventually have to adapt to
an outdoor enclosure, as well as become the companion to a
new and somewhat unpredictable chimpanzee. The day began
with the Danish veterinary authorities declaring her free of
salmonella and tuberculosis before she then had to take leave
with her keepers, who were sad about losing her, before finally
being put into a provisional travel cage and transported to
Kastrup Airport. Three rows of seats had been removed from
the Maersk Air DK 0228 from Copenhagen to make space for
Miff's cage. The airline flew Miff for free as a part of a sponsor-
ship agreement and Captain Jens Hald respectfully welcomed
her aboard in "monkey business class." The flight attendants
served her fruit when the other passengers got their coffee,
and later that evening, on April 23, she landed on Norwegian
soil at Kjevik Airport. Edvard Moseid met the party at the
airport. He tried to take a look at Miff through the cage bars,
but she stuck her hand out and promptly punched him in the
face.[202] Moseid interpreted this as a good sign.

Exhausted from her journey and very stressed from the
change of surroundings, Miff was driven straight to the zoo

and released into a sleeping pen where she gathered straw to make herself a small nest and soon settled down to catch up on her rest. But Julius was only two sleeping pens away and could smell the new female chimpanzee. He kept her awake with whoops and bangs until she had finally reached her limit and hit the wall with a tremendous smack. Her reaction worked. Julius fell quiet and the keepers observing the interaction took this as a good sign, too. Maybe Miff would have the guts and the vigor needed to be a good match for Julius.[203]

Media interest in Julius had been waning for quite a long time, but this new change of events blew up into a PR and media comeback that is unique in the history of the Norwegian entertainment industry. The zoo had played its hand well. The entire press corps of Norway was informed about the date and time that Miff would be picked up in Copenhagen, and when she would arrive at Kjevik Airport. The largest tabloid, VG, was granted exclusive access on the flight. The zookeepers in Copenhagen were astonished when a throng of press people showed up to cover the transport of a chimpanzee.[204] VG expressed their gratitude for the exclusive story by covering the event with grandeur enough for a royal wedding. On her first morning in Norway, Miff's photograph flanked the entire front page, and the story of her transport filled a double spread inside the nation's largest newspaper. The TV2 and NRK channels told her story during their evening news features that evening. Even the Danish papers were caught up in the enthusiasm: "Danish-Norwegian Ape-Romance," declared the headlines in the Danish newspaper, Berlingske Tidende, and gave Erik Eriksen, the veterinarian of the Copenhagen Zoological Garden, the honor of explaining to the Danish population why all of Norway was so enthralled by the transport of this particular chimpanzee. "Julius is extremely popular in Norway—it's almost as if the crown prince was getting himself a girl," he explained, not knowing that the Norwegian Telegraph Agency had just sent its royal court reporter to cover the Julius story in the coming days.[205]

Miff would have ten days to acclimatize to the zoo before meeting Julius. After four days, Miff was led alone into the Julius Grotto for the first time. Julius was outside, and she was able to explore and inspect the area. After a while, she gathered a bit of fresh straw and lay down in a corner for a nap. Miff's behavioral patterns were clearly different than those of the Kristiansand chimpanzees. She had several human traits, such as "politely" holding her hand in front of her mouth when she yawned, refusing to peel her own bananas and being picky about her food and drink.

On May 5, 1996, at 1:30 p.m., Miff was scheduled to meet Julius. A variety of national news media and several hundred children and adults showed up to bear witness. "The ape romance of the century in Kristiansand Zoo was attended by the majority of the southern capital's upper crust," wrote *Dagbladet*.[206] The mayor of Kristiansand, Bjørg Wallevik, officially opened the Julius Grotto, first wishing the married couple "luck and success" before the doors were opened so that both animals could enter the area. Julius didn't waste a moment establishing his territory. The guests were allowed to throw bananas into the enclosure in celebration of the big day. Julius showed his appreciation by tearing up flowers and plants from his pen and tossing them back toward the public.

Miff stayed well inside her safe pen. The zoo had done a small test run earlier in the day, opening the door but not pressuring Miff. She soon went out but received a shock when she touched the electric fence, which along with the moat, made the enclosure escape-proof. Now she chose to stay in her pen and peek out at the island and the people during the festivities. "I am sure everything will be fine once they have spent a few days together," Edvard Moseid comforted the crowd and the press.[207] When Miff finally took a few tentative steps into the enclosure, Julius rushed at her, showing her who was in charge and frightening her. Miff was startled and urinated on herself before sauntering back to her pen.

So many things were foreign to Miff. She had never before been outside before, and on this day, the weather was cold and bitter. There were crowds of people and a lot of racket, and in addition, an intimidating male chimpanzee who was intent on marking his territory. Of course, the newspapers interpreted everything in human terms as the PR work surrounding Julius had encouraged: "Julius is no hen-pecked man, and made it immediately clear that in this marriage there would never be gender equality," VG concluded.[208]

MIFF'S SURPRISE

Over the next days, the two chimpanzees were put together in the Julius Grotto where they mostly remained at a distance and observed one another. Even though it was May, it was still cold enough outside that the zookeepers worried Miff might get sick if she went outside.[209] One week passed before Miff was allowed to venture outdoors. She was skeptical. Julius first had to go outside alone before she dared to follow him. Grete Svendsen rewarded her with pre-peeled bananas when she returned back inside.

Their island was situated so that they could look directly across the water at the other chimpanzees when they were all outside. On May 13, both groups were released outside and the other chimpanzees had a chance to see Miff for the first time. The other chimpanzees found the new arrival exciting, even if they couldn't do anything other than call to each other and toss things from island to island. Miff and Julius continued sleeping in separate pens at night but spent their days together. As May progressed, Julius and Miff gradually became more familiar with each other. It appeared that Miff was more interested in contact with him than the other way around. "He is not angry with her, it's more as if she was nothing but air to him," Svendsen explained.[210] After a while, Billy was put in with Julius and Miff. The plan was for these three to form the core of the new community.

It was taking longer than expected for Miff to ovulate, and the zookeepers speculated about whether her cycle was irregular because she was still so young or whether the delay was due to her stressful move from Copenhagen to Kristiansand. In any case, Julius and Miff had not had any sexual contact. Toward the end of the month, they finally had their first physical contact; Julius smacked Miff several times on the back. To the public this action might appear hostile, but Arne Magne Robstad believed it was an expression "that they value one another."[211]

A long time had passed since Julius had received as much media attention as he did in this particular week. When it came to PR, Moseid had once again hit the nail on the head. Throughout two weeks in May, while families across Norway were planning their summer vacations, daily ads featured the romance of Julius and Miff. The theologian, Eyvind Skeie, published a children's book about Julius in 1996, telling the story of his life from birth up until his meeting with Miff. "The marriage" with Miff was written as a kind of long-desired happy ending after a life of turbulence. "Now he stands in a corner of the Monkey Grotto. He has trees and stones to look at, rocks to climb and water. And there is Miff. Two chimpanzees meet. A new time has begun," were the five last lines in the book.[212]

But reality once again failed to comply. It was not so easy to make this fading fairy tale about the human chimpanzee Julius rise from the ashes. Miff continued to be on her guard around Julius. She still wasn't ovulating and had not yet been in heat nor been sexually available for him. After thirty-eight days on Norwegian soil, only three weeks after the official grand wedding celebration, her keepers were surprised to discover the explanation for Miff's reservations. On the afternoon of Thursday, May 30, 1996, something remarkable happened. One of the zoo employees walking past the Julius Grotto at 6:00 p.m. noticed Miff bleeding and hastily informed Edvard Moseid that something was wrong. Moseid was in his office and thought that Miff must have been hurt. He rushed down to the Julius Grotto and arrived just in time to be the shocked witness of Miff giving birth to a tiny male chimpanzee.[213]

In other words, Miff had been seven months pregnant when she was moved to Norway. No one in Copenhagen or Kristiansand had noticed anything until the morning that Miff was discovered with an infant on her lap. Testing chimpanzees for pregnancy is quite simple. One can use the same tools and methods as for humans: a urine test and two straight lines determine pregnancy. But nobody had thought to test Miff. She had no apparent belly, and her newborn weighed only about 2 pounds.[214]

The birth went well. Miff knew exactly what to do, carrying the tiny infant and placenta, finding a new clean spot, washing and drying him with a bit of straw and allowing the umbilical cord to hang and to fall off on its own.[215] Normally, the zoo would wait to announce new births until everything seemed to be stable, but the carpenters working on the final touches of the Julius Grotto had observed what was going on, and it would soon be impossible to keep the story under wraps. On May 31, Moseid decided to cancel all his appointments and prepare for another moment of national media attention. He sent off a press release via fax to all of the news agencies. It took just three minutes from the time his fax went through the machine until the phone started to ring.[216] The story was broadcast in daily news briefings on NRK's radio station several times throughout the day. Moseid didn't try to cover up the manner in which the news had taken him and the zoo by surprise: "I admit it's a bit embarrassing, but we didn't have any idea about this."[217] The zookeepers assumed that Julius must have been quick to figure out the situation and seen what none of the humans had seen, and this may have been the reason why he was so apathetic toward Miff.

Officially, the zoo communicated its joy about the birth: "We are celebrating. Our intention with the Julius Grotto was to build up a new chimpanzee family. This is a much quicker start than we could have imagined," the zoo's chief Robstad said in a public statement.[218] But Robstad wasn't being honest. The zoo was not celebrating. For observers and the media—and therefore also the zoo—the grand Julius narrative was essential. It might now be three or four years before Miff would be able to become pregnant again. And the newborn's genetic makeup might turn out to be weak and even the result of inbreeding. Both Miff's father and brother had made sexual advances toward her in Copenhagen, *VG* told the public, adding that it was "far from a scandal. This is totally normal in the chimp world."[219]

But this isn't true. The chimpanzee species would have long since buckled under natural selection if inbreeding between a father and daughter was commonplace. Sex between a mother and son is also very rare. Although Jane Goodall has observed such behavior, it takes quite a lot of pressure from the son and is often met with strong resistance from the mother. Sex between a father and daughter is usually avoided because male chimpanzees tent to be attracted to older females. This preference has developed as an indirect protection against incest. Male chimpanzees cannot know which young are their own within a community, and by preferring to mate with females of their own age or older, it becomes impossible for their partners to be their own daughters.[220]

The entire Miff story was comical and paradoxical for the press. In the zoo world, however, there was nothing too unusual about it. It is simply quite difficult to see when a female chimpanzee is pregnant even when she is near the end of her term. But, after the entire media of Norway had covered the story in the manner of a royal wedding, it was a mind-bending exercise to suddenly normalize the case and let monkeys be monkeys. The entire ordeal was staged as a public pageant. The show must go on. *VG* ran coverage of the story by referring to paternity law, which presumes that a wife's husband is the legal father to a child, regardless of whether it is his own biological child or that of another father. The story caused even Jarle Madsen, the former head of F2F, a Norwegian organization working to ensure the presence of both parents in a child's life following a divorce, to comment on the surprising birth and application of paternity law in this particular case: Madsen felt it was unjust for the biological father in Denmark to lose his paternity rights and this further demonstrated that the entire law should be scrapped.[221]

BABY IN THE WATER

Miff proved to be a good mother. She carried her baby close to her body all day long. Julius and Billy were kept separate from her and the baby. They raced around Julius Island while Miff and the nameless infant remained inside in the Julius Grotto.

If nothing else, the complications raised public attention for the zoo. After the miserable deficit of 1995, a new record for visitors to the zoo was set in 1996 with 520,000 guests, an increase of over 20 percent.[222]

Over the summer, the zoo attempted to reunite Miff and Julius. On Thursday, July 11, Julius and Billy were put in together with Miff and the baby for the first time. While Julius had acted indifferently toward Miff when they were first introduced, he was now more aggressive and persistent. They both screamed, challenging and even sometimes biting one another, though not enough that their keepers felt things were out of control and instead perceived the situation as normal chimpanzee behavior.[223] On the next day, another attempt was made to reunite them, but this time Julius went completely berserk. He ran around and struck Miff so that she dropped her six-week-old infant into the water. The keepers had to rush in and push Julius away with a high-powered hose to get him into an isolation cage. Arne Magne Robstad came running and found the infant still floating facedown in the water. He carried the baby chimpanzee out of the enclosure, placed his mouth over the chimp's tiny mouth and nose and gave him mouth-to-mouth resuscitation while simultaneously attempting to massage his heart back into rhythm. He had never before administered live-saving first aid to a chimpanzee but it worked. After fifteen minutes, the infant began breathing again.[224]

The keepers were tense and worried about whether Miff would accept the baby back. Another rejection and a new Julius complication was the last thing they needed. At first, Miff seemed uninterested and left the baby to lie alone on the ground, but then she decided to pick him up and resume her mothering.

It was hard to know whether Julius had acted intentionally to hurt the baby or whether it was an accident. But to kill an infant that is not one's own biological offspring would in fact, evolutionarily speaking, be reasonable. If her infant were to die, Miff would be in heat much sooner, further increasing the chances that Julius would be able to spread his genes. Chimpanzees don't reason in this way, of course, but this is the evolutionary explanation for why infanticide is relatively widespread among many species when a new leader assumes the alpha role and does not have much reason to believe that he is the biological father to any of the young. As much as 38 percent of infant deaths among gorillas are the result of murder.[225] The biologist Martin Daly and the psychologist Margo Wilson claim that this mechanism even applies to humans and that it is statistically a hundred times more likely for a human child to be murdered by a stepfather than by a biological father.[226]

Miff's tiny baby appeared revived, but his condition was still critical. The water that had been in his lungs could cause pneumonia, and baby chimpanzees are not very resilient against infections. The fifteen minutes without breathing may also have resulted in brain damage. His permanent condition was extremely uncertain for several days. He was lethargic but conscious. Zoo staff kept close watch over him, but chose to leave him with his mother instead of removing him for closer medical attention, since doing so would risk his rejection by Miff.

In the public Julius narrative, this event was difficult to place. Edvard Moseid had to defend Julius: "Julius is not a child murderer," he explained. He was simply a little too "rough and arrogant."[227] The natural brutality between chimpanzees always had to be downplayed to the public. The fact that Dennis had truly murdered poor Skinny by throwing her by the foot against a concrete wall and splitting her skull was never mentioned. Julius's story couldn't handle any such hints of savagery. Julius was almost human, and any story, and the public perception of him had to be along those lines. The official explanation was that Julius didn't mean any harm; he was merely clumsy because he'd had a different upbringing.

Any idea of reuniting Miff and Julius was delayed for a while. Julius and Billy would have to get along on their own.

Up until now, Edvard Moseid had been dealt an unbelievably lucky hand with the media coverage surrounding Julius. All of the difficulties with isolation, the cage, escape attempts and safety deviations had either been hushed up or trivialized. But it was getting more and more difficult to rewrite Julius's fate with a good PR-spin. Several newspapers began to openly critique the zoo's treatment of Julius. One correspondent in *Dagbladet* thought that the only solution was to euthanize "the psychopath chimpanzee Julius."[228] Gunvald Opstad, with *Fædrelandsvennen*, was of the opinion that the zoo was abusing both Julius and Miff for commercial gain. "The management should have come to realize by now that the male chimpanzee Julius is a frustrated and wayward being whose existence has been utterly destroyed," he wrote, accusing the zoo of "exploiting these poor misaligned animals most shamefully for advertisement."[229]

It was becoming quite the feat to imagine how Julius could ever integrate harmoniously into a community of chimpanzees. What had once been a sweet and child-friendly story about Julius the chimpanzee had morphed into a tragedy. In the Aristotelian theory of tragedy, the protagonist follows a trajectory from a happy to an unhappy condition via a dramatic turning point, in which he comes to a realization about himself and must thereafter meet his inevitable fate. The course of Julius's life seemed to be running uncomfortably close to Aristotle's poetics: He had been happy as a small creature among humans. Back in his chimp community, he had perhaps realized that he would never belong in either world. His current phase was part of his painfully long fall into isolation and loneliness.

"HE'S LIMP BUT WE'RE
KEEPING AN EYE ON HIM"

After two weeks, the zoo was able to breathe a sigh of relief and conclude that Miff's baby had hardly suffered any permanent damage as a result of the "accident." The public was invited to submit names. A surprising number of entrants had suggested "Moses," and so in the end, this name was chosen. It was both a nod to Edvard Moseid and a sign that bible-savvy southern Norwegians knew the name Moses meant: "drawn out of the water."

In the fall of 1996, Julius and Miff took turns spending time in the Julius Grotto. Julius and Billy were allowed in for few hours, and then Miff and Moses were released in on their own. In 1997, Miff and Moses were released into the main chimpanzee enclosure with the other group, while Billy and Julius were left like two frustrated bachelors in the Julius Grotto. The idea was that Miff would be returned again once Moses was old enough for her to start ovulating again. Moses still clung to his mother; he was a weak baby and never fully regained his strength after the mishap. On December 19, 1997, he died. The post-mortem could not find a direct cause of death, and so it was declared a natural death. The timing, however, could not have been more terrible. One week later, on December 26, 1997, Julius would turn eighteen years old. Although the animal Julius was having a tragic life, it was still possible to conjure up life events and excitement around the fictional Julius. His birthday had been planned as a gigantic PR-hype. The zoo decided to delay the story of Moses's death so as not to put a damper on the festivities. An entire production was arranged around the idea of Julius coming of age and being old enough to drive. A car dealer gifted Julius a car—following the tradition of the Norwegian royal family children receiving cars at the age of eighteen. The inspector at the Kristiansand Traffic Services, Kjell Larsen, even went along and issued a bona fide driver's license for Julius. The National Agency for Motor Vehicles later heard about the false license and demanded that zoo chief Arne Magne Robstad send the document to Oslo to be destroyed.[230]

Over 1,000 guests showed up for the celebration. They got to see Julius eat cream cake and drink soda pop and open and peel birthday bananas. Media coverage was once again overwhelming. The country's largest newspapers came to Kristiansand, and TV2 ran a feature on their news hour that same evening. A journalist from *Agderposten*, Tor Martin Lien, who closely followed zoo-related stories and knew of Moses's weak condition, asked Arne Magne Robstad during the festivities how the little creature was doing. "He's limp but we're keeping an eye on him," Robstad replied.[231]

"Moses had been dead for three days by that point. No wonder he was limp," the journalist Lien later commented when the news of Moses's death was released the following week.[232] The zoo hadn't admitted to the death until December 31. TV2 reported that Julius's stepson had died of natural causes. It was Miff's first baby, and not unusual for chimpanzee mothers to fail at raising their firstborns, was the explanation. But to the outside world it felt as though Julius was cursed. He had escaped five times and had been put into isolation. He had fathered two babies with Josefine, both of whom had died, one during the birth and one of illness two years later. He had been given his own grotto and a specially-imported wife from Denmark who turned out to be pregnant on arrival. And he had nearly killed her baby, which now one year later, had died "of natural causes."

The public Julius narrative had devolved into a tangled up mess. First, he was presented as in being love with Josefine, then as a possible father to Bini's stillborn baby, then returned to monogamy with Josefine again, only to have an almost royal wedding with the pregnant "virgin" Miff. Now his step-son was dead and buried in secret so as not to ruin the mood at his eighteenth birthday party. The whole thing was comical in a macabre way. It was four weddings and a funeral.

The silver lining in an otherwise dark cloud, if one is some-what cynical, was that following the death of her baby, Miff would be in heat much sooner, allowing for the possibility of bringing Julius and Miff together once more. "Though we haven't yet created a concrete strategy, the death of course does accelerate our process of bringing Miff and Julius back together," said Arne Magne Robstad.[233]

It would once again be up to him.

Chapter 9

THE CHILD

"Chimpanzees are incredibly tolerant of infants."[234]

FRANS DE WAAL

U P UNTIL THE moment when the bubble suddenly burst, Edvard Moseid had actually succeeded in reviving Julius's celebrity status. For a short period, media attention was back at its 1983 levels before it fell silent once more. The marriage between Julius and Miff was down the drain; he was no one's father, nor was he the member of a community. The newspapers found other things to write about, and it seemed people were tired of the whole Julius affair. He slid into a more anonymous existence.

Miff and Julius were once again put together in an enclosure, but this time the media was not informed. Since Moses was dead and Miff was no longer a nursing mother, she was free to start ovulating and become fertile once more. Finally, the zoo would have a chance to see whether Julius and Miff might have their own baby. The two of them did well together and didn't show any hostility toward one another. However, they also didn't show much interest. Time passed, Miff went into heat but never got pregnant while living together with Julius.

The whole point of the costly Julius Grotto and Julius Island project was to help Julius father his own young and to establish a family. There were limits to how long the zoo could wait. They decided to try putting him together with other female chimpanzees. In the spring of 1999, while Julius and Billy were together in the Julius Grotto, the zoo decided to experiment by releasing Josefine, Julius's "former girlfriend" inside. After all, Josefine had become pregnant twice with him. Even if both babies had died, the pregnancies still proved that the two of them could be a good match.

The last time they had been together, Josefine had tended to be a bit too subservient toward Julius, but her temperament had since changed completely. She was aggressive and angry and bold and totally unafraid. She bossed around the two male chimpanzees, took control of the situation and was uninterested in mating. At first, the keepers interpreted her behavior as a kind of long-planned revenge for the way that Julius had treated her when she was younger. But the keepers eventually realized that her behavior had medical reasons. They discovered cysts in her pelvic area and believed these must be causing her to suffer from a hormonal disorder that made her abnormally aggressive. "She is suffering from hormonal disorders and believes she is a man. Which includes teaching Julius some manners," Edvard Moseid explained.[235]

In the meanwhile, the bizarre Julius Prize had shifted focus. It was no longer awarded to Norwegian pop artists but to individuals or organizations engaging in human, animal or nature conservation. In 1998, the prize was given to chimpanzee researcher and activist Jane Goodall. She had an incredibly busy schedule, and Moseid met her as she traveled through Sweden in order to hand her the sculptor Peter Valeur's bronze Julius statue and a check worth $6,500 USD. Goodall planned to use the money for the Sweetwaters Chimpanzee Sanctuary in Kenya. This was a reservation for lone chimpanzees whose mothers had being shot or captured alive. The goal was to foster these orphans in such a way that they could eventually be released and survive in the wild.

It was not until the year 2000 that Goodall was able to come visit the Kristiansand Zoo for her celebration. She spent half a day walking around in the park. She was able to see Julius for the first time up close—one of the world's most famous chimpanzees meeting the world's most famous chimpanzee researcher. Goodall was not principally opposed to zoos. She believed that it depended on the zoo as well as what alternative fate the animals might have had. Many wild chimpanzees live in ruined natural conditions and in such constant fear of humans that Goodall believed they might be better off in modern zoos.[236]

Jane Goodall liked what she saw in Kristiansand. She got to hear the entire strange history of Julius. In principle, she did not like chimpanzees to be brought up among humans. However, she understood that the zoo had not had a choice in the matter.[237] Many of the zoo employees were starstruck upon meeting her. Both the Glad and Moseid families had read Goodall's books from cover to cover. The previous year, Moseid had resigned as director of the zoo after thirty-two years of service, twenty of them while suffering from serious health problems. Now, he dreamed of moving to Kenya to work as a volunteer on Goodall's reservation. And when Dixi had a young female chimpanzee with Champis in November of 1999, she was of course called "Jane."

Only a few months later, in April 2000, Miff bore a small male chimpanzee by the name of Knerten. Jane and Knerten were both fathered by Champis and were genetic half-siblings. They were to grow up together and be more generally amicable and content than the half-brother duo Billy and Julius. While the main group lived in harmony, both Billy and Julius still lived alone. Chimpanzees are communal animals, made to live in larger groups. Julius was clearly disturbed and thrown off by his situation, and it was impossible to hide his frustrations from the public. "Julius has become so vicious and grumpy," said the new zoo director, Reidar Fuglestad, in a public remark.[238] Julius's birthday, the day after Christmas, was celebrated as usual with soda and cake and the press and fans. But he didn't look particularly happy during the celebrations, and *Agderposten* was unable to produce the usual upbeat story that they had printed so many times previously about the charming, intelligent chimpanzee. "The many children in attendance were greeted with a screaming, restless chimpanzee who is unable to find peace even at the age of 21," the newspaper correspondent wrote.[239]

JULIUS JUNIOR II

In March, Bini gave birth to a small male chimpanzee. The baby was fathered by Champis, of course. It was the third time she had given birth. Neither of the first two infants had survived, and after only a week, this one died as well. Bini rapidly came into heat once again, and the zoo decided to try putting her together with Julius every time she was ovulating. Anything could happen, they speculated. The meeting, however, went surprisingly well. Bini and Julius accepted each other, and he was able to mate with her. After that, the zoo decided that Bini would come visiting whenever she was in heat, and after a period of time, she became pregnant by Julius. The pregnancy was kept under wraps this time, since she had lost three babies before, and no one expected it to go well. On April 12, 2002, Bini gave birth to a little female chimpanzee, but she died of malnourishment after only five days.[240]

This was Bini's fourth pregnancy, and the fourth baby she had lost. With this loss, Julius had by now fathered and lost three of his own babies as well as his stepson, Moses. Still, Bini and Julius were so agreeable together that the zoo decided to make them a permanent pair in the Julius Grotto. There would no longer be space for Billy, however. Billy and Julius were both strong adult males now and were often in fights. Julius held the upper hand on Billy, but both had the ability to hurt the other. Billy once gave Julius a ghastly bite on his head.[241]

It's not easy for multiple male chimpanzees to live together. The Royal Burgers' Zoo in Arnhem is among the zoos that allows for this, and has thus seen several times how brutal it can be. A male chimpanzee named Luit, who had won dominance over his community through the long fight that Frans de Waal portrayed in *Chimpanzee Politics*, was later made to pay the highest price for his exposed position as alpha leader. The community's former leader, Yeroen, had managed to win over Luit's next in command, Nikkie, convincing him to switch sides, and one night they both carried out a coordinated murder of Luit. The staff had noticed that something was amiss on the previous evening, but they were unable to lure the three chimpanzees into separate pens for the night. When they returned to the zoo the next morning, Yeroen and Nikkie were unhurt, but Luit lay in a pool of blood with his head toward the fence, still alive but with his toes and fingers bitten off, wounds covering his entire body and massive blood loss. His life could not be saved. Upon closer inspection, the keepers were able to see that his testicles had been bitten and extracted from his body.[242]

The Kristiansand Zoo could not risk scenes such as this. Especially not where Norway's most beloved animal was concerned. There was simply no space for both Julius and Billy. Time was up. Relocating an adult male chimpanzee to another zoo was practically impossible. The only solution was to put Billy down. Julius was the priority; it was "survival of the cutest." Wider society finds it hard to accept the euthanization of a healthy animal, but it is impossible for a zoo to function otherwise. It is a common enough occurrence; it simply isn't announced in any press releases. Not even Billy's namesake, Billy Glad, was informed of what had happened. The chimpanzee Billy vanished silently from the saga.[243]

Just as silently—and some years prior—Kjell had also been put down. But there had been medical reasons behind his death. His congenital bone disease had developed into a hip deformity that he was unable to live with.

Julius was now left alone with Bini. He no longer had to fight with Billy when Bini was in heat. She was pregnant again in no time. But it wasn't her fertility that was the problem, so the zoo wisely kept quiet about her condition once more. On May 15, 2003, ten years to the day on which Julius had fathered Julius Junior with Josefine, Bini secretly gave birth to a small male chimpanzee. The birth went without a hitch and Bini didn't require any help, but none of the keepers expected it to go well since Bini had lost all of her previous young. Her keepers left her alone, but when the young chimpanzee was still alive after two weeks, they started to feel a twinge of hope that perhaps things might turn out differently this time. In any case, they continued to keep their distance and let Bini carry on with her mothering. After three weeks they still had not gone into the enclosure to confirm the animal's gender.[244]

The media attention paid to this birth was much less than that with which Julius had been showered. His pop star status was diminishing, and his fan club had grown used to all of his babies dying. In addition, the timing was not optimal since the zoo's first tiger pair, Ulysses and Ryeka, had just given birth to a female tiger named Tinka on the same day. It was the first tiger birth on Norwegian soil, and since Ryeka was a first-time mother and proved to be somewhat ignorant, the zookeeper Rune Landås was put in charge of feeding Tinka milk from a bottle. This made for a good photo op. It was Tinka and not Julius's new baby that drew families to visit the zoo in the summer of 2003.

It wasn't until June 4, 2003, that the zoo released the news that Julius had finally become a father to a chimpanzee who would most likely grow up. This had been the goal ever since Josefine had arrived from Sweden sixteen years earlier: for Julius to become a father and to have his own family among the chimpanzee group. And because Julius was Julius, both TV2 and NRK cleared space for the story in their news programs that evening.

The Julius family stayed together throughout the infancy. Julius accepted the young chimpanzee and didn't interfere. Bini had learned from her bitter experiences and was finally able to provide enough milk for the baby to grow stronger. The zoo waited to name the infant until they felt even more confident that things would go well, but once it was clear that he would be fine, and since he was a boy, the name practically took care of itself. They did what they had done before and named him Julius Junior. If the brand was under threat, it was important to cultivate and strengthen the brand name.

A LONELY ARTIST

Fædrelandsvennen tried to call Edvard Moseid to congratulate him on the birth of Julius Junior but they couldn't reach him. Moseid had, in fact, made good on his word and moved to Kenya. He was now living at the Jane Goodall Sweetwaters Sanctuary just west of the 17,057-foot-high Mount Kenya. Chimpanzees did not used to inhabit Kenya. They lived in the rain forest, primarily in Central Africa. But with the culling of the rainforest, the natural surroundings also disappeared. Humans hunted the animals too, both as trophy food for unscrupulous, wealthy bigwigs and as attractions in circuses and private homes. Goodall's workers scoured the world confiscating such abused animals. Thus far, twenty-five chimpanzees had been released into the reservation. Moseid was connected to the project as an advisor and volunteer. He cared for and changed the diapers of baby chimpanzees, and he trained them to stay together in groups. He drew from his experience with Julius to help chimpanzees that would one day have to survive in the wild. Moseid saw this as a duty he owed after his years with Julius.[245]

Several of the chimpanzee keepers and zoo employees were actively engaged in this and other similar projects. It was hard to sit quietly in Norway knowing that the existence of wild chimpanzees was being threatened. But the work was costly and required private contributions. The zoo came up with the idea of Julius contributing to the cause by collecting donations for the project. Why couldn't Julius create a series of paintings to be sold at an exhibition, with the proceeds going to Jane Goodall's project? After all, he had painted as a small chimp when he used to live with the Moseid family, sitting on the floor with the girls and learning to hold a brush and paint. The artist, Peter Valeur, and the zookeeper, Åse Sundbø, helped Julius to prepare. Sitting in front of the bars of Julius's sleeping pen, they held up the canvas, brushes and cups of paint. Julius himself could choose the colors and paint whatever he wished. He typically spent between three and five minutes per painting, but every now and then, he would focus for a full fifteen minutes. He enjoyed creating two to three paintings in a single round but didn't seem to have much of a sense for when a painting was finished or not. Peter Valeur would say "stop" whenever he believed a composition was perfect.

On some days, Julius was more interested in eating the paint than in drawing with it. Other days he appeared to enjoy the activity. Every now and then, a selection of press members would be allowed in to observe the session, but then Julius would often become distracted and more interested in the strangers than in his work. He also didn't like Peter Valeur, especially not when Valeur had the idea to play the jaw harp in order to inspire Julius. Julius wasn't about to have a damned jaw harp anywhere near his cage and threw his enormous chimpanzee body up against the bars in protest.[246]

By Easter 2004, Julius had produced a large enough port-folio of paintings to arrange his first exhibit. Easter Thursday was the formal preview. The seasoned art auctioneer from Grev Wedels Plass Auctions, Hans Richard Elgheim, was impressed by Julius's art: "My first reaction is that the pictures are original, an amazing concept," said Elgheim.[247] The zoo laid their cards perfectly in introducing Julius as an artist. They produced only a limited number of prints, and all of the paint-ings were numbered and accompanied by a signed certificate of authenticity. The art was potentially valuable but unusually easy to counterfeit, so the originals had to be given this extra validation. The first painting went for $1,300. Within a year, Julius had raised $9,000 for his fellow brethren in Africa by selling twenty-three different paintings.[248]

Julius was by no means the first chimpanzee to make art. There are many examples of captive chimpanzees who enjoy artistic activities. Several of them even do it independently of any praise or encouragement from humans.[249] The chim-panzee Congo, from the London Zoo, is perhaps the most well-known chimpanzee artist of them all with his own exhi-bition at the Royal Festival Hall in 1958, the most prestigious art arena for any international artist. Pablo Picasso was among those who bought one of Congo's 400 works. But while chim-panzee art happens as a result of human initiative, there are also many examples in the animal world of what one might call an early stage or evolutionary stage phenomenon of what we humans refer to as art.[250] Elephants are among the species that might choose to draw in the sand with their trunks, while the so-called garden bird, or bowerbird, in New Guinea is truly the most extreme example of an animal artist. Male birds of this species built huts to attract mates, and these huts are such impressive structures that random passersby will assume humans have constructed them. The huts are seven to ten feet in diameter and over three feet high, often with green moss in front of the entrance and adorned with hundreds of decorations such as flowers, fruit, leaves, mushrooms and butterfly wings. The birds group objects of the same color together, and some of the huts are even painted with crushed leaves or oil from the leaves. The entire incredible structure is built to impress a mate, and this system is not such a bad idea. If a female chooses a male with an impressive hut, there is a lot she already knows about the genetic material of her future co-parent. She knows that he must be strong enough to have built a hut many times larger than himself, that he has the mechanical abilities needed to weave together several hundred twigs into the shape of a hut, that he has a good mind that can sort a variety of objects into categories by color, that he has good eyesight and a good memory for finding all of the many elements needed, and that he, in general, must be a bird that is able to master life, since he has managed to stay alive for long enough to perfect all of these skills. In addition, she knows that he must be dominant over his rivals because these birds, of course, also spend a lot of time trying to destroy other birds' huts.[251]

Julius in the hands of a human. *(Photo: Billy Glad)*

Julius in bed with Ane Moseid.
(Photo: Arild Jackobsen)

Zoo director Edvard Moseid—
with a kangaroo in his shirt.
(Photo: Fædrelandsvennen)

Julius, bandaged, has been given painkillers and is resting in the bathroom. *(Photo: Billy Glad)*

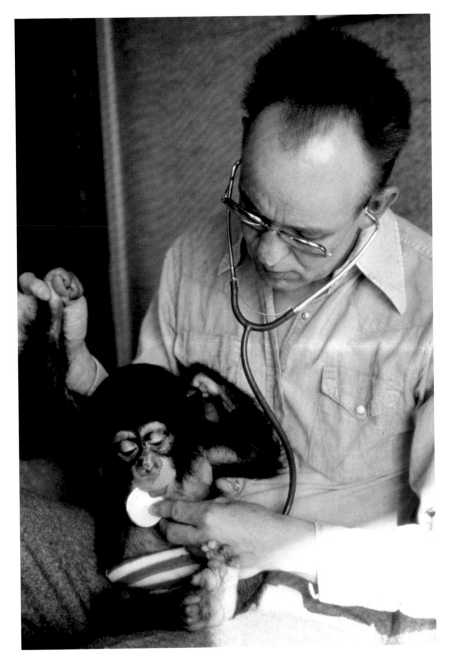

Billy Glad examines Julius. *(Photo: Reidun Glad)*

Ane Moseid teaches Julius to paint. *(Photo: Arild Jakobsen)*

Julius on a boat trip with Reidun Glad. *(Photo: Billy Glad)*

Julius plays with Carl Christian Glad. *(Photo: Billy Glad)*

Marit Moseid gives Julius a bottle. *(Photo: Arild Jakobsen)*

Birthday celebration with his "human siblings." *(Photo: Arild Jakobsen)*

Julius in the cage. *(Photo: Arild Jakobsen)*

Edvard Moseid introduces Julius to Chimp Island. *(Photo: Arild Jakobsen)*

Julius poses at a photo shoot for a children's book. *(Photo: Arild Jakobsen)*

The Tropical House fire on August 2, 1978. Director Moseid is running by on the right. *(Photo:* Fædrelandsvennen*)*

Billy and Kjell in the Tropical House with their mothers—Julius (right) is on his own. *(Photo: Arild Jakobsen)*

Ane and Siv play on Chimp Island with Julius. *(Photo: Arild Jakobsen)*

Julius climbs out through the roof. *(Photo: Knut Uppstad/VG/NTB Scanpix)*

Julius escapes from the chimp enclosure and into the zoo. The guests are unaware of the potential danger. *(Photo: Knut Uppstad/VG/NTB Scanpix)*

Julius is confined to an escape-proof cage. *(Photo: Helge Mikalsen/VG/NTB Scanpix)*

Julius (right) and Miff (left) in the Julius Grotto. *(Photo: Arild Jakobsen)*

Julius Junior. *(Photo: Kristiansand Zoo)*

Left to right: Julius, Josefine, and Billy. *(Photo: Nicolai Prebensen/VG/ NTB Scanpix)*

Julius's art. *(Photo: Hans Martin Sveindal)*

Julius—almost 45 pounds overweight. *(Photo: Nicolai Prebensen/VG/ NTB Scanpix)*

Julius celebrates his thirtieth birthday. *(Photo: Hans Martin Sveindal)*

King Julius.
(Photo: Kristiansand Zoo)

There are evolutionary reasons why art can have an important meaning in the animal kingdom. There are animals that are able to decorate a structure with colors and objects that appear beautiful to the human eye. Could it be that the animals themselves view it as beautiful? Could it be that even Julius is able to see something as beautiful? Could it be that he enjoys painting in a way that is similar to the pleasure a human artist takes in their work? The keepers that helped the chimpanzee Congo to paint reported that he was able to work for long periods at a time, that he would get enraged when his brushes and colors were taken away and that he had an obvious sense of symmetry in his paintings and a clear opinion about when a picture was finished.[252] Julius was less attached to such things. Perhaps he lacked Congo's talent. In any case, the keepers responsible for the Julius brand clearly were happy for this art project. It was a full-on PR feast. It gave an ironic kick to contemporary art. It served as a reminder of Julius's incredible skills. And it was a charitable act.

But when Edvard Moseid returned from Africa in time for the exhibit, he was shocked at the sight of Julius. Moseid had recently spent a lot of time around scrawny chimpanzees in Kenya. He hadn't seen Julius for a long time and was of the opinion that the chimpanzee had grown alarmingly heavy. Moseid didn't hold back when he was interviewed: "He's fat. Disturbingly fat, in my opinion. I know I am hurting some by saying so, but compared to the chimpanzees we have in Kenya, he is double the size. I've had my own share of heart problems, so I can say that he should not be so fat," said Moseid.[253]

The zoo didn't even try to brush off the criticism from its original patriarch: "There's no point in denying that Julius is too fat. We are going to do something about it," admitted Arne Magne Robstad, reporting that Julius had been put on a diet.[254] Julius now weighed between 175 and 200 pounds, roughly 45 pounds more than he should. Until further notice, he would have to forego all bananas. He was given yogurt for breakfast, dry fodder with vitamins and minerals for lunch and vegetables for dinner.

The cause of Julius's weight gain had a lot to do with Julius Junior. Bini was nursing and therefore required large amounts of food. Junior was starting to eat solid foods in addition to his mother's milk, and they were served their meals together in the Julius Grotto. If the family were separated for meals, they would have to be apart for several hours a day, risking adjustment difficulties between the three of them. The problem with meals together, however, was that Julius took too much of the food for himself. This meant that the trio was given even larger portions, resulting in Julius taking even larger amounts and growing much too heavy. Chimpanzees in the wild are usually good at sharing food resulting from a hunt, but they are terrible at sharing fruit. Such behavior is presumably because the hunt requires cooperation, in which multiple group members contribute to the catch. There are clearly defined tasks—some surround the prey, others close off potential escape routes, while others are responsible for the attack. If a chimp wishes to partake and to be allowed in on good hunting opportunities in the future, it is important to understand that everyone is entitled to a portion of the catch. But chancing across a large amount of fruit does not presuppose such collaboration in the same manner, and so the regulations for sharing do not apply.[255] Julius now had access to enormous quantities of food, but he did not have any instinct that the food should be shared or any other principles of hunting justice, even though it was his own son with whom he should be sharing. He ate and ate and grew more and more plump. His keepers disliked the development but didn't know how to adjust his intake. After six months of dieting, there wasn't even the slightest change when it was time for Julius to weigh in.[256]

Julius was just as fat and happy. If viewed from the outside, his success as an artist, as well as his fortunate pairing with Bini, not to mention becoming a father to Junior, might all seem like a welcome upswing in his life. Finally he had had his baby. After an eternity of bad luck, stillbirths and setbacks, the zoo had succeeded. But the family project was, in truth, more important for the brand and the fictional figure Julius than for the animal himself. In reality, paternity is not a strong bond for chimpanzees. Integration in a community is much more significant. Chimpanzees are social animals. For several decades, Julius had been without a community. An isolated chimpanzee is not a truly fulfilled chimpanzee, even if he has both a wife and a child and a surplus of food. His outside island was separated from the other chimpanzee island by a moat. He could look across to the others who got to live with the group; he could look over at his rival Champis who strutted around with all his ladies. Julius must have hated Champis. They would often roar at each other. In the wild they would have long since fought one another. Here, a mere few feet of water held them in check. For now.

Chapter 10

KING OF THE APES

"Uneasy lies the head that wears a crown."[257]
WILLIAM SHAKESPEARE

WHILE JULIUS HAD grown steadily larger, Champis steadily diminished. Champis, who had once been so robust and strong and in love with food, was increasingly thin and scrawny. At only the age of thirty, his teeth were rotting, his urine stank, and he was often out of breath and weak. It turned out that he had diabetes. If he had been healthy, it would be possible for Champis to live for many years to come but his situation was going downhill. He was soon only a shadow of his proud community leader self, and so the zoo decided to put him down. This was good news and a window of opportunity for Julius, as the alpha male position was now vacant, and all of the other competing adult chimpanzees were gone. Kjell, Billy and Champis had all been put down, as had Jesper, Dixi's oldest son. Tobias and Knerten were still too young to be rivals. Julius was already on a positive trajectory since he was now a successful partner to Bini and a father to Julius Junior. Could he now possibly rejoin the chimp community as their leader? If so, it would be the ideal conclusion to his muddled life, a surprising happy ending after a life of chaos.

Many of his keepers thought the idea was unrealistic. As a chimpanzee, they believed Julius was too much of a misfit. He had lived for so long in isolation from the main group that they felt he would never be able to make it as a leader. He didn't know anything about life among a chimpanzee community, they argued. But keeper Rune Landås, who had recently become team leader for the Ape Jungle, believed in the project and was undeterred by the slew of objections. Landås had an unusual knack for discerning animal behavior, having grown up closely among animals and managing his farm in Vennesla when he wasn't at the zoo. He was also currently fostering the two-year-old tiger female, Tinka, in addition to his position as team leader for the Ape Jungle. He couldn't bear the thought of Julius continuing to live a separated life away from the rest of the community. As nice as the Julius Grotto and Julius Island enclosures were, Julius remained socially miserable. He had far too little interaction with other chimpanzees and far too few social challenges. He had become temperamental, almost manic from the social deficit. Rune Landås could not support subjecting as intelligent and social an animal as Julius to another decade away from his group. The only solution was for Julius to return to the community. And to do so, he would have to enter it as their leader. This was his chance.[258]

Along with veterinarian Rolf Arne Ølberg, Landås drew up an elaborate plan for reintegration. The various enclosures were adapted and remodeled. The Ape Jungle was closed to the public for over a month during the secret integration process. Julius was about to face the toughest challenge of his life. Becoming a group leader is a difficult task, and it is an equally difficult position to maintain. A chimpanzee community is an advanced social system. In natural conditions, a community is usually made up of twenty to fifty individuals. Within a single group of fifty chimps, there are 1,225 one-to-one relationships and countless other possible social combinations.[259] Alliances and oppositions are constantly formed and rivalry and conflict are common occurrences. The job of the alpha male is to keep the peace without becoming unpopular. The chimpanzee community in Kristiansand was, by these standards, unnaturally small and not as complex. But the requirements for a group leader are higher and different than for a ranking member of the unit. An alpha male must be unbiased whenever he interferes and breaks up conflicts. One of the reasons that wild chimpanzee communities are always led by males is that, without fail, females favor their own young in conflicts. By contrast, it's impossible for male chimpanzees to know whether a young chimp is their own offspring or someone else's, allowing them the ability to rise above such blood alliances. The intended alpha position for Julius would be demanding. And it still wasn't clear whether the other chimpanzees would accept him as their leader. The worst-case scenario would be if the female chimpanzees joined forces to kill him. Although females don't have the canine teeth of males, Rune Landås believed they could easily kill Julius if they worked together.[260]

For the past few years, Julius, Bini and Junior had lived together in the Julius Grotto. The first step in the integration process was to release the three of them into the Ape Jungle and allow them to become familiar with the area while the other chimpanzees were in their sleeping quarters. The only time that Julius had ever been released into this enclosure was for a short period ten years prior. Chimpanzees are territorial creatures; Julius sniffed, observed and soon understood that he had been put into another group's territory. He became aggressive and agitated, patrolling the area. Rune Landås had prepped the enclosure by spreading nuts and fruit around in order to create a positive experience for the three nervous chimpanzees. Junior clung to Bini's back while Julius stood on his hind legs in the middle of the enclosure and whooped. All three were jumpy, but after a while, they calmed down and appeared to be enjoying themselves. They helped themselves to the food and tried out all of their new climbing options. They were given free rein of the large enclosure, and it wasn't until the seventh day that two other chimpanzees were released in to join them.[261]

ONE ON ONE

Dixi and her daughter, Jane, were the first two to come in. Rune Landås and Rolf Arne Ølberg were sober-minded southern Norwegians, but even they were on tenterhooks to see what would happen. Ølberg stood by, prepared with anesthetic darts. Dixi was a powerful chimpanzee, two years older than Julius and a veteran member of the Kristiansand community for almost twenty years. At first, Julius behaved cautiously passive when the two chimpanzees entered, but then he pulled himself together and started to behave more aggressively and gruff, even toward Bini and his own son Junior. It was an effective reaction. To become the alpha male of the community, he would have to demonstrate that he was able to boss everyone around. Julius then unceremoniously went about trying to mate with Dixi. Dixi was ovulating on that day, and though the zookeepers had not exactly planned for something like this to happen when they had drafted their reintegration plan, it was a fortunate coincidence. It meant that Julius found Dixi particularly interesting. After Dixi immediately acquiesced to Julius, it wasn't long before they had mated for the first time. Meanwhile, Jane had started playing with Junior. Junior wasn't used to other chimpanzees, and so the fact that he quickly caught on and began to play with another older individual was an extremely promising start.[262]

The next day, an additional pair was let in to join Dixi, Jane, Julius, Bini and Junior: Julius's "ex-wife" Miff and her son, Knerten. Bini immediately initiated bodily contact with Miff. But then Dixi suddenly began to attack Julius. On the previous day, Dixi had been submissive to Julius, but as soon as the community numbers grew, the dynamic shifted and Dixi decided to challenge him. She chased him around. Miff watched what was happening and decided to throw herself into an alliance with Dixi, pursuing Julius around the enclosure. Miff bit his foot. It appeared as if Julius had lost respect. But then, all at once, all was calm again. It was hard for the keepers to see and understand why things had quieted down so quickly. But Julius had won. The others had given up.

Tobias was the penultimate chimpanzee to rejoin the group. He was the son of Dixi and Champis and thus, strictly speaking, heir to the alpha crown and a potential challenger.

On top of that, he was almost thirteen years old, not socially mature, but older than both Dennis and Champis had been when they had assumed leadership. If Tobias were to pick a fight upon entering, the previous uprising when Miff bit Julius indicated that the others might be tempted to go along with him. But Tobias was afraid himself. It was a scary thing to enter alone into a new community where a hierarchy of sorts had already been established. Rune Landås and Rolf Arne Ølberg had ranked each of the chimpanzees from one to nine. Each time another chimpanzee was released into the enclosure, it was always a lower ranked chimpanzee who entered next. In this way, they made sure that it would be difficult for the newcomer to challenge Julius, presuming that all of the others already present had accepted him. The process went according to plan. Tobias slid into the group and found his place without any conflict. Eight of the chimpanzees were now allowed a period of time to get used to each other.

Josefine was the final chimpanzee remaining in the sleeping quarters. The decision to put her in at the end was very deliberate. Josefine was the one Landås and Ølberg feared most. By showing up last to the party, after everyone else had already gotten into the groove, they hoped it would be especially hard for her to instigate a rebellion. They degraded her status in order to increase Julius's odds. This did not rule out the possibility, however, that Josefine might still be able to wreck an entire month of work and a twenty-year-old dream.

The keepers kept close watch on the interactions between the community members. During their lunch and coffee breaks, they sat beside a live TV stream of the Ape Jungle. Every time they saw there was tension in the air, they readied the fire extinguishers. In such charged conditions, the water hoses the keepers normally used wouldn't be effective enough to separate the chimpanzees, and though the zoo had never used fire extinguishers against chimpanzees, other zoos had suggested that the CO_2 powder in these devices would be effective in completely paralyzing the chimpanzees in conflict situations.

Josefine's entrance shifted the dynamic. The group quickly split into two. Julius, Bini and Junior against the rest. It was the new group against the old community or, from a territorial perspective, the Julius Grotto versus the Ape Jungle. The old community was larger and on their own turf. Together, they turned on the three newcomers and pressed them backward. Julius, Bini and Junior backed up further and further until they could do nothing but stand there and scream—literally with their backs up against the wall. Julius howled and turned to look despairingly toward Rune Landås, who was watching from the public viewing platform. If Julius didn't counterattack, he would appear to concede defeat. He could not lead a community by displaying fear. Landås and Ølberg had no plan B. The thought of removing Julius from the community once again and making him start all over in the Julius Grotto was unbearable. Julius would have to fend for himself. He may not get any other chances if the other chimpanzees realized how weak he could be. This was the moment that would define the rest of his life. Jane, Tobias and Knerten supported Josefine's attack. Then, Julius appeared to abruptly make up his mind. He suddenly flashed his teeth and stormed toward the others, challenging them one by one and driving them backward. Josefine lost her allies and suddenly found herself as the one being chased and backed up against the wall. None of the chimpanzees came to blows, but Julius had proven that he was ready to fight for his position. He had displayed courage and won their respect. After that, he was quick to reconcile with all of the chimpanzees. At long last, he had become a worthy leader of a chimpanzee community.[263]

ON TOP OF THE WORLD

Landås and Ølberg had succeeded in what many did not think was possible. The entire community group had accepted Julius as their leader, and all of the chimpanzees could now be together without any more squabbles and racket. Julius now knew what was expected of him. It was as if he had been unemployed for his entire adult life and had just been installed as the administrative director of Chimpanzee Community, Inc. Julius could celebrate his twenty-sixth birthday that year as the alpha male leader. It was too good to be true. "Julius is finally the king of the apes," wrote *Dagbladet*.[264] The old Julius Grotto and Julius Island were history. A troop of spider monkeys were installed in those enclosures. From now on there would only be one group of chimpanzees living in Kristiansand. And Julius was their boss. The first period proved to be a steep learning curve, but Julius intuited what he needed to do in order to keep the other chimpanzee's respect without being too harsh. He was able to interfere effectively whenever community tensions arose and before they turned into full-blown conflicts.

The entire situation was divine. There was no one lording over him, there was no one to challenge him, he was served his food, he had no external enemies to threaten his territory, he had five adult female chimpanzees at his disposal and enjoyed regular sex with all five. Tobias and Knerten were castrated and Junior was a child so Julius had a harem all to himself. Chimpanzees are not shy when they mate, which they often do in front of the other community members. However, there is a strange trait shared by all chimpanzee communities, both in the wild and in captivity, namely that their young always try to intervene whenever they see adults mating. The young chimpanzees might, for example, climb up onto the backs of the copulating pair and attempt to pull them apart. The behavior is so universal that it can only be explained in evolutionary terms as a behavioral pattern, which increases a young chimp's chance of survival by reducing the chances for new individuals—and new competitors for limited resources and motherly care—to be born. All the more remarkable is to see how tolerant the adult males are with these outbursts from the young chimpanzees. Males gingerly lift the children off their backs and try to finish their business. They are most likely so tolerant because any reprisals toward the young might result in opposing reactions from the mothers, which could trigger further conflicts in the group.[265]

Julius Junior acted like every other chimpanzee child, climbing onto his father's back whenever he got close to an ovulating female. Julius Senior was like all the other chimpanzee fathers and kindly, but decisively, lifted his son off again and tried to finish. After all, finishing didn't take that much time. By March of 2006, Dixi was pregnant. On the morning of Sunday, November 5, the keepers discovered that she had given birth to a little chimpanzee baby. All of the chimpanzees stood in a circle around Dixi to watch the newborn until the keepers arrived.[266] Julius was a father once more, to another boy as it turned out. Dixi took good care of him. A name competition was held again and people could vote online. The popular name, Linus, won first place, with Dennis, in honor of his grandfather, coming in second.[267]

Julius turned out to be a surprisingly good father. The chimpanzee world has clear gender roles. Females are responsible for looking after and bringing up the children while the males compete to lead the group and are responsible for protecting the territory against outside enemies. There are certainly exceptions to this rule, and there are examples showing that it's possible to break these patterns if conditions so require. Male chimpanzees, for instance, have also been observed assuming "motherly duties" for motherless chimpanzees.[268] But in general, chimpanzees organize themselves not unlike the family structures of Western humans in the 1950s. Chimpanzee children have a tendency to play differently depending on their gender. Both small male and female chimpanzees might play with sticks that they have picked up, but it is only the young females who carry the sticks around like little dolls. Wild female chimpanzees might go the whole day carrying these sticks, bring them to sleep at night and build small nests to place them in, but no one has ever observed a young male chimpanzee engaging in similar behavior.[269]

It is nonetheless impossible to draw conclusions from the way that chimpanzees organize themselves in order to determine how humans should organize. If, for no other reason, than there is another species of chimpanzee which is as close to humans genetically and evolutionarily as the common chimpanzee but which organizes its social structure in a completely different manner. The lesser-known, smaller chimpanzee species, the bonobo or the pygmy chimpanzee, which was first discovered and categorized as its own species in 1929, is as close a relative to humans as the common chimpanzee. But the behavior of bonobos is radically different than that of common chimps in some very important ways. Bonobos are not very violent. The males are not the decision-makers; they do not spend much time hunting and tend to have few conflicts and a great deal of sex. They have been called "left bank chimpanzees" partially because they dwell on the opposite side of the Congo River than the other chimpanzees and gorillas, but also because there is something socialistic about the organization of their social system. Although bonobos are group animals like chimpanzees, it is the females who pilot the community in a shared leadership team together with other females. While common chimpanzee males must balance a double-edged alliance with each other—on the one hand cooperating to find food and protect the territory and on the other competing internally for a spot in the hierarchy and thereby the right to mate—male bonobos are never rivals. They are a remarkably peaceful and empathetic species. New brain research studies of bonobos have supported claims made by observers of these primates in the wild that portions of their brains which register the suffering of others are larger in bonobos' brains than in those of chimpanzees. Bonobos, quite simply, are empathetic animals.[270]

Bonobos have sex in the human missionary position, but they also go for a host of other more impressive varieties, for example hanging upside down by one's feet. And sex is not only tied to the reproductive phase as it is among chimpanzees. Bonobos also have sex during infertile periods and they often have same-gendered sex. Male chimpanzees masturbate one another and female bonobos often lie stomach to stomach, rubbing their genitals together. Researchers have not been able to find any exclusively heterosexual or exclusively homosexual bonobos; they are all bisexual. This free sexual development creates more peaceful conditions in the relationships between adult individuals. While sex is a constant source of conflict among chimpanzees, the bonobos are able to sidestep the topic altogether. And, what's more, such liberal sexuality creates safer conditions for growing young bonobos. There are several species in which a new leader will quickly kill many or all of the young in the group since they do not belong to him, genetically speaking. But because the bonobos are always sleeping with each other, it is impossible for them to divide the troop's young between one's own and someone else's. Everyone collaborates to protect and assist the youngest members until they reach a reproductive age. Infanticide is well documented among chimpanzees, gorillas and humans, but not among bonobos. In fact, it has never been observed, neither in captivity nor in the wild.[271]

SETTING THE ANIMAL FREE

Julius, however, was better than your typical chimpanzee papa. He was as far from ignorant as it's possible to be. He took clear delight in playing and spending time with his children, especially with Junior, who had turned into a frisky and active three-year-old. Often, Junior would sit in front of his father and stretch his long chimpanzee arms up and around his neck. Julius was also much more tolerant and indulgent than normal chimpanzee fathers. Could it be that he remembered his upbringing among the Norwegian fathers of the late 1970s, Billy Glad and Edvard Moseid?[272]

These were glorious days. Julius was a respectful chief in the community and had finally come into his own family with two healthy sons that would most likely live to adulthood. But he also had a twenty-year-old brother in Thailand whose fate was not as rosy.

Most Norwegians had long forgotten about this brother, but in 2007, a surprising reminder popped up in several of the country's newspapers. The young male named Mardon, born to Julius's mother Sanne in 1987, was still alive and living in Thailand. Together with Bastian, he had been sent from Kristiansand to Öland Zoo in Sweden in exchange for Josefine. There he had been renamed Ola and, like Julius, had lived a relatively turbulent life. When he was only one and a half, the Öland Zoo had lent Ola out to a theater in Stockholm for a production of August Strindberg's *Gustav III*. While in this role, he lived at the home of artist Louise Tillberg and actor Stephan Karlsén and their three children. Every evening, Karlsén drove Ola to the theater, dressed him in a costume and carried him to the side stage where, twenty minutes into the third act, he was taken onstage by lead actor Ingvar Hirdwall, who was playing Gustav III. Once onstage, Ola was paraded around to the astonished squeals of audience members before being led offstage again and driven back home by Karlsén and put to bed.[273] The scene impressed people. Ola was a staunch little actor and took part in eighty-one shows. He later got roles in two films and a few commercials before finally returning to the Öland Zoo. He lived with the Tillberg–Karlsén family from September 30, 1988 until May 25, 1989. A children's TV series broadcast on Swedish television was based on the couple's own home videos from their life with Ola. Louise Tillberg subsequently published several children's books about the little "Chimpanzee Ola." He became a TV star and a children's book subject just like his brother had, but in 1995, when he was eight years old, Öland Zoo decided to sell him to the Safari World zoo in Bangkok, Thailand. Ola's new conditions were extremely wretched. He was kept in a cement cage, shared with three other chimpanzees, that was just 150 square feet in size. This treatment was pure animal torture, and the Tillberg–Karlsén family advocated to change his situation. They visited him twice in Thailand, which caused a media storm in Sweden. People began to arrange demonstrations for Ola, and even the Swedish State Department and the Swedish royal family got engaged on his behalf, but to no avail. Then, the Norwegian animal protection organization NOAH had heard about the case. When they quickly realized Ola's connection to Julius and the Kristiansand Zoo, it was not hard to sell the news story to the papers. "It is gross neglect for the Kristiansand Zoo to dismiss responsibility for Ola," said NOAH's leader, Siri Martinsen.[274] The goal was to have Ola transferred to one of the African rehabilitation centers, such as Jane Goodall's, which work with abused chimpanzees.

Boris Bravin, the Öland Zoo owner at the time when Ola had been sold, thought the Ola activists were demonizing and exaggerating the situation: "The photo of Ola is of his sleeping pen. In the daytime, he and the others share a

800–900-square-foot pen. This is perhaps not good enough for Norwegian standards, but it's a lot better than many other zoos around the world."[275] The case reached coverage on all of Norway's largest news media. *VG* immediately dispatched a journalist to Bangkok to see Ola's conditions first hand but found the cage empty. No one at the zoo was willing to talk to Norwegian reporters. *VG* stayed in Bangkok for several days but was unable to uncover any clues about Ola's fate.[276]

The new Kristiansand Zoo director, Per Arnstein Aamot, was sad to hear about Ola: "This was twenty years ago. We are trying to find out whether he is doing well, and we are sad when we learn that animals are not kept in good conditions," he responded to NOAH's criticism. The Kristiansand Zoo is a member of the European Association of Zoos and Aquaria (EAZA) that organizes the exchange of animals between parks and ensures satisfactory conditions for animals in all member parks.[277] A chimpanzee would never have been sanctioned to be held under such conditions in an EAZA-approved zoo.

Proper care and treatment of the animals and of their needs was increasingly becoming the primary goal for any serious zoo. Ola's life would have been much better had he remained in Kristiansand. But even with the improved chimpanzee facilities in Kristiansand, which had become more elaborate and modern, there were still those who were unwilling to tolerate chimpanzees living in captivity. Julius's old human mother, Marit Espejord (formerly Moseid), was unable to visit Julius at the zoo without getting a knot in her stomach. There was something off about it. She never said this in public, but she had always felt it was wrong for Julius to be in a zoo. He didn't belong there, not even after finally becoming an integrated community member and the alpha male. She thought he was much too smart to spend his life being gawked at by human children, though she was, of course, clear that there were no other alternatives as Julius had been born in the zoo.[278] He could not live among humans. And he would be completely helpless if he were set loose in the jungle.

Many people are of the opinion that chimpanzees don't belong in zoos. In his book, *Rattling the Cage*, U.S. animal rights lawyer Steven Wise questions why chimpanzees, who are thinking, self-aware creatures, are not treated lawfully as humans instead of as things. In 1993, the Australian moral philosopher, Peter Singer, and the Italian animal rights activist, Paola Cavalieri, founded the Great Ape Project. The project, which is still ongoing, aims to secure basic legal rights for chimpanzees, gorillas and orangutans, such as the right to live, the right to freedom and the right to protection from torture. In other words, humans should stop using these animals for research or for display in zoos. As early as 1975, Singer coined the phrase "animal liberation" as the next liberation movement, following women's liberation and African American liberation. Singer thinks that even the term "animal" does more to conceal than to reveal: "In the popular mind the term 'animal' lumps together beings as different as oysters and chimpanzees, while placing a gulf between chimpanzees and humans, although our relationship to those apes is much closer than the oyster's."[279]

To counter this viewpoint, one may argue that the work of zoos, such as the one in Kristiansand, is increasingly more vital in keeping living specimens of species that are becoming extinct in the wild. Wild chimpanzees live exclusively in West and Central Africa, north of the Congo River from Guinea to Uganda. They stick to the jungle areas, but their populations have dwindled so dramatically over the last century that chimpanzees are now listed as an endangered species, meaning that the future of their existence is grave. Hunters, deadly illnesses and the destruction of their habitats are among the primary threats.

One should also not romanticize the everyday natural conditions of wild chimpanzees. Jane Goodall admitted that she did this for a long time. During her first years with wild chimpanzees, living among them and observing their daily habits, she viewed them as more noble creatures than humans. Chimpanzees were peace-loving beings, she believed, who cooperated and interacted harmoniously, looked out for one another and spent the majority of their time grooming and cuddling. And that was that. It was only after ten years of observing chimpanzee behavior that Goodall made some discoveries that rattled her and raised awareness among animal researchers worldwide.

Since 1970, the chimpanzee community she had studied at Gombe had begun to split itself up. By 1972, it had become two clearly delineated groups, geographically and socially: one community lived north in Kasakela and the other lived south in Kahama. They shared a small margin of overlapping territory, but they always slept in separate locations. Over time, they began interacting less and less frequently, and starting in early 1974, Goodall and her research colleagues began to register the first confrontations between the two groups. After a while, they observed that a veritable war had broken out. The Kasakela chimpanzees had more numbers and were stronger.

They had eight adult male chimpanzees and controlled a territory spanning six square miles. In January 1974, six of the adult males, one teenager and one ovulating adult female from Kasakela ventured south into the Kahama territory. Here they encountered the chimpanzee Godi. He tried to flee, but the group was able to catch and hold him by the leg, and while one of them held him down on the ground, the others went wild, beating him as hard as they could. They kept at it for ten minutes and concluded by throwing an enormous rock at Godi before running off in triumph and leaving the creature lying on the ground with life-threatening injuries. After this attack, Godi vanished and was never seen again.[280] One month later, a new attack was recorded and similar onslaughts occurred in the years that followed. These were chimpanzees who had once belonged to the same community, who had moved and hunted together and slept in close quarters for years, who had shared long grooming and delousing sessions in each other's arms, who were now savagely inflicting harm on each other. And these attacks were not for the purpose of securing hunts or hierarchical positions or limited resources, rather they were carried out purely as territorial war. Within a few years, the Kasakela chimpanzees would completely wipe out the members of the Kahama community. Their raids were disturbingly brutal. Even if their victims did not put up a fight and merely curled up to save their lives, the beatings could go on for a long time and involve several perpetrators with the clear aim of hurting the victim and inflicting pain. In February 1975, the Kahama chimpanzee, Goliath, was murdered by his former community friends. He had grown old and weary and unable to protect himself and could do nothing but lie with his arms over his head while a group of Kasakela chimpanzees jumped on him beat him, twisted his legs to break them both, hit and dragged him back and forth on the ground.[281] By 1978, the war was over. The Kasakela community had won. All of the male Kahama chimpanzees had been slaughtered, and their females had been killed or fled to other communities or switched over to the side of the champions. From 1978 on, the Kasakela chimpanzees slept freely in the old Kahama territory as a symbol of their victory.

This war was by no means exceptional. Similar territorial wars between different chimpanzee communities have since been observed in other regions. In addition, around the same period when they recorded this territorial conflict, Jane Goodall and her colleagues also discovered a series of cannibalistic attacks among chimpanzee mothers in a community group that were just as disturbing. They noticed that Passion, an adult female and Pom, her daughter, were working together to kidnap, kill and eat the babies of other mothers in the community. From 1974 to 1977, they observed the pair killing and eating three small chimpanzee babies. Circumstantial evidence, however, indicates that the duo in likelihood caught and ate up to ten young chimpanzees during this period.[282]

Some of these strikes were described in detail by Goodall's research group. On one November day in 1976, for example, Passion viciously assailed another female chimpanzee mother Melissa and her three-week-old infant, Genie. The onslaught began at 5:10 p.m., Passion and Pom coordinated as always— Passion pummeling Melissa relentlessly for ten minutes, pinning her to the ground and biting her face and hands, while Pom attempted to wrench the baby from her arms. After two minutes, blood ran from Melissa's upper lip and Passion was able to grab Genie, but Melissa succeeded in saving her baby by biting Passion's hands. Passion stood upright, went around behind Melissa and attacked her again with a hard bite on her rump. Melissa ignored the pain and continued to fend off Pom in order to keep her grasp of Genie. Meanwhile, Passion started in on her hands, which were clinging to the baby. She bit each finger one by one, and Pom was able to push in and bite the three-week-old infant hard on the head. Melissa still refused to let go, but Passion pulled her onto her back, placed a foot on her chest and ripped the baby free. Pom took off with her prey and climbed a tree with the baby, which had most likely already died from its injuries, and Passion followed her. Melissa tried to get up but collapsed from her wounds and remained lying on the ground, while Passion and Pom sat in the tree eating her baby.

Three minutes later, Melissa was able to stand on her legs and climb up to Passion and Pom and the dead chimpanzee. Passion and Pom rebuffed her but no longer aggressively. Melissa pulled back but then tried again several more times. Melissa's rump was bleeding profusely and her face was torn up, but now she sought out contact with Passion—in that strange manner of chimpanzees who wish to be quickly reconciled after a conflict. She climbed up the tree, and they held hands until Melissa retreated. Twelve minutes later, she returned once more, and Passion warmly took hold of Melissa's injured hand and gazed deeply into her eyes, while continuing to gnaw on the remains of her baby.[283]

Nature is extraordinarily brutal. Chimpanzees can eat each other's babies directly in front of the mother's mournful eyes.

They can even comfort the mother of the baby that they are still eating. Chimpanzees can battle for territory, target, pre-meditate and intentionally murder old friends and relatives, slowly and painfully. Julius was fortunate to have avoided all of this. In the wild, wars are commonplace, but in the artificial surroundings of the zoo, peace is king. Julius lives in a shielded world and is subjected to less pain and fear than he ever would have faced in the wild. He is able to forego the savage degradation that every single alpha male in the wild must inevitably face. He will never starve because he is served food on a regular schedule. He receives medical attention and painkillers whenever necessary. He is provided with a regimen of stimulating activities and challenges. He doesn't know that there are chimpanzees living freely in the jungles of Africa. He has never been outside of Norway. Perhaps he is happy.

Chapter 11

END GAME

"Chimpanzees never make an uncalculated move."[284]

FRANS DE WAAL

ON DECEMBER 26, 2009, Julius turned thirty years old. His birthday celebrations had become an important part of the zoo's brand, but from a commercial perspective, celebrating during the Christmas season was problematic. His thirtieth birthday party was therefore moved to October 8th, a time of year when it was still possible for chimpanzees to be outside in Norway. All 400 daycares in the district were invited and 1,400 children in total showed up. Julius was served cake, soda pop and gifts just like in the old days. The children were served buns, juice and a good amount of Julius stories to bring back home.[285] This birthday party was reminiscent of the once-popular but controversial "chimpanzee tea parties" that so many zoos used to arrange. The London Zoo, in particular, was known for gatherings in which the chimpanzees were dressed up like humans and positioned around a finely decked table and served tea.[286] The tradition began in 1926 and continued up until 1972, only seven years before Julius entered the world. The difference between the tea parties and Julius's birthday celebrations was that he clearly seemed to be enjoying them. Sugar and attention were his two favorite things. He whooped wildly when he was let out onto Chimp Island and saw that a party had been prepared. The joyful whoop of chimpanzees can be high pitched and frightening, but people familiar with the animals are able to identify it. He hopped onto the table and helped himself to marzipan cake, drank a gallon of soda and tore open his gifts which were, among other things, a painting canvas, pictures and clothes.[287] Julius showed off with his usual party tricks: while the other chimpanzees had to bite off the top of the soda bottle to get a drink, Julius was able to elegantly screw off the cap.

Just before Christmas, as his actual birthday drew near, another party was held with his closest family members and former keepers. He was still able to remember the faces and voices of everyone who had meant something to him. Edvard Moseid could be standing behind a throng of a hundred people gathered around Julius's enclosure on a summer day, but the moment Moseid calls to him, Julius immediately hears and recognizes whom the voice belongs to. He even recognizes Ane and Siv Moseid when they come to visit Chimp Island, even though they were only four and two years old when Julius lived with them and have since grown up. Whenever he sees them, he indicates a desire to play all their old games and goes down to stand at the edge of the moat looking up at them on the other side, signaling that they should play tag. He shifts his weight from one foot to the other while waiting for the start signal and is just as paranoid that no one should cheat as when he was a little chimp.[288]

In general, chimpanzees have exceptional memories. Experiments show that their memories are in fact eidetic, or photographic, and their ability to recognize faces is astonishing.[289] Their ability to recognize voices is even better. The natural rainforest habitat of chimpanzees has thick vegetation and bad visibility, so within the social structure of a community that lives and works together across a large territory, they primarily use their voices to let others know where they are. Although Julius is now an integrated community member and alpha male, and even though he hasn't left his enclosure for almost twenty-five years, he still remembers both the voices and faces of those people who meant something to him as a child. Every time his old friends come to visit, the experience is clearly very touching for him. He often acts strangely when those closest to him arrive for a visit. If it has been more than two months since their last visit, he will at first act upset. He sits with his back to them and looks sulky until he suddenly changes his mood, becomes animated and goes on a series of impressive loops around the enclosure. After that, he prefers to be more intimate, sitting up as close as he can get to the glass or the bars in his old sleeping cage. It can almost seem as if Julius deliberately plays at acting upset, in order to make his guests feel guilty for staying away too long.

Chimpanzees can be very good actors. As social and self-conscious animals, they understand how they appear in the eyes of other chimpanzees and thus how they need to appear in order to achieve their aims. Chimpanzees perform while other group members look on. The two male chimpanzees Yeroen and Nikkie from the Arnhem zoo in the Netherlands, who had formed an alliance to kill their rival, Luit, once got into a fight with one another. Nikkie bit Yeroen's foot and Yeroen began to limp for several days. After this, the researchers observed something strange. They noticed that Yeroen continued to limp even after his injury had healed, but only whenever Nikkie was watching him. As soon as Nikkie was elsewhere, he ran around effortlessly. This observation was so fascinating that they set up a full team of observers in order to verify the behavior. Yeroen's acting turned out to be very effective. He played the injured party each time Nikkie saw him, perhaps in order to win sympathy, perhaps in order to avoid further rough handling or perhaps to remind Nikkie that wounding his friend and ally was not the smartest thing to do.[290] If Yeroen was able to act injured, it is not unlikely that Julius might pretend to be sad every time he is reminded of his traumatic upbringing, as though to rub bad consciences into the faces of his human friends.

A BIRTH IN THE RAIN

Julius's thirtieth birthday celebration was a reminder of his prominent status in the human world. But otherwise he was now less human than ever before. He was getting along well within his community. He shared a particularly good bond with Jane, the now almost adult and fully sexually mature chimpanzee, who had been named after Jane Goodall. Julius and Jane mated often whenever she was in heat, sometimes with young Linus clambering around on their backs. Jane got pregnant and gave birth to a stillborn baby. But she was soon pregnant again, and on Tuesday, September 6, 2011, she gave birth outdoors during a terrible rainstorm. She climbed up into a small tree house on Chimp Island. Jane thought it was a perfectly cozy place to give birth. The keepers didn't quite agree; chimpanzees are not made to give birth outdoors in Norway in September. It wouldn't take much for a small newborn to catch pneumonia. The birth was without complications, but the downpour continued and Jane decided to lie down inside the hut with the baby. The zoo employees manically checked the weather reports online. A dry patch was predicted to soon arrive, and so they waited and hoped and were afraid that they would be too late. They debated doping Jane with a dart so that they could go out onto the island and take the baby away from her and bring him inside. Then the storm broke up. The pouring rain turned to a light drizzle, and Jane picked up the infant and ran inside to get warm.[291] The baby, who turned out to be a female chimpanzee, was later given the name Yr, which means drizzle.

Ironically, Julius had so far fathered children with Bini, Dixi and Jane. In other words, the only two female chimpanzees with whom he had *not* had any young were the two he had publicly "married" in all the newspapers and tabloids: Josefine and Miff. Both Jane and Julius had been born at the zoo. Yr's birth marked the second generation of Kristiansand chimpanzees. Of the four grandparents—Sanne, Dennis, Champis and Dixi—only Dixi was still alive. Relationships can easily get tangled up in a small community. Dixi was the mother of Linus and Jane and the grandmother of Yr. Julius was the father of both Linus and Yr, and Linus was therefore both an uncle and a half-brother to Yr.

Less public attention was paid to this birth than to previous ones. Julius was no longer as popular as he had once been. This was his third child so the event no longer felt as significant to the public, and in any case, in September of 2011, Norway was still in shock following the terrorist attack that had taken place on Utøya Island on July 22. Nothing in the country was as it was before. Curiosity about newborn chimpanzees suddenly seemed far away and unimportant.

Julius had become the father of three babies. Yr was healthy and continued to grow but had to put up with some rough-housing from other young chimpanzees. Knerten and Junior thought a baby was fun and enjoyed running around with her as if she were a doll. Yr easily got tired out from the game and wasn't able to get any sleep, and Jane, seeing that such games were unhealthy for her daughter, appealed to Julius to inter-vene with the young chimpanzees. But in this case, Julius was a dysfunctional leader. He was never strict enough with the young chimpanzees, and it almost seemed as if Knerten and Junior were using Yr to test their limits. The test showed that their limits were quite elastic.[292]

With Yr in the group, Linus was no longer the center of attention as he had been for the past five years. On the evening of May 3, 2012, he suddenly vanished. Rune Landås quickly noticed that something was not right when he went to let the chimpanzees in. The mood among the group was extremely strange; they were all very calm and crossed the bridge from Ape Jungle to the inside enclosure in silence. One by one they quietly passed by but Linus was not among them. Landås searched high and low across the island but could not find a trace of him. He feared that Linus may have fallen into the moat and drowned. He suspected that Linus may have slid down the slippery grass and into the water near the hut where he liked to play. Landås put on waders and looked around in the water. He didn't find anything, gave up for the evening and went home. The next morning he continued his search, putting on his waders once again and walking around in the moat, while feeling with his feet. In the water just outside the wood hut, his feet touched something soft. He bent down and lifted up Linus's dead body. Landås stood at a loss with the chimpanzee corpse in his hands. Without thinking, he gently stroked the coat of the young chimpanzee before wrapping him in a burlap sack and carrying him out.[293]

Stillborn babies and young who were unable to survive had become the norm in this particular chimp community. However this was something else entirely. Linus had been a focal point for five years, and they had all been together day in and day out. And now, all of a sudden, he was gone. None of the other chimpanzees got to see the body. Perhaps they understood that he was dead, and perhaps some of them had witnessed him fall into the water. Nonetheless, when the chimps came out onto Chimp Island the following day, they looked for Linus. Julius sat staring at the water. The community was uneasy over the next few days. It was apparent in observing Julius and the others that Linus was missing. There was a somber mood among the group, Landås thought. Dixi sat often by herself and did not want to go outside.[294]

Throughout his lifetime, Julius experienced many deaths. He had survived Dennis, Bølla, Lotta, Sanne, Kjell, Jesper, Billy and Champis. In addition to all of the stillbirths, he had also seen baby Moses, Julius Junior and now young Linus die. And many other young chimpanzees—such as his brother Mardon (Ola)—had been taken out of the community and vanished for good. As mentioned earlier, chimpanzees clearly seem to understand what death is, but it has not been concluded whether this means that chimpanzees realize the reality of their own deaths and that they will also die someday. At the Primate Research Institute at the University of Kyoto in Japan, the chimpanzee Rio was paralyzed from his neck down after a spinal inflammation. He was given around-the-clock care and was able to eat and drink much the same as before, but he could not move his body. In the wild, he would have died but neither his mood nor his attitude toward life ever seemed depressed. He remained just as good-natured as always. He provoked the research students by spitting water at them as he had always done. He was neither fearful nor agitated about his future.[295] His strangely unaltered behavior made the researchers speculate that perhaps Rio simply did not understand that he would die and that chimpanzees may live under the sublime belief that they will never die themselves, even if they see the deaths of others around them.

Similarly, one can only speculate about what Julius himself thinks about his future and his life. We know that chimpanzees are socially advanced animals, that they are self-conscious and have large brains. In studying the ratio of brains to body weight among the animal kingdom, one could reasonably expect a chimpanzee brain to weigh 5 ounces, when in fact it weighs in at 400 grams 14 ounces. Intellectually, chimpanzees are over-equipped relative to their daily nourishment requirements. Since chimpanzees are social animals and enter into intricate and shifting alliances, rivalries and enemy relationships with other individuals, they must be able to think strategically and comprehensively, including evaluating others' intentions, masking their own intentions, making complex decisions and making plans for the future. This social situation has resulted in an abnormally large brain. But whether or not chimpanzees are also able to use this over-equipped brain capacity to ruminate on their own deaths, and whether Julius understands that his heart will one day stop beating, we will never truly know.

BINI'S DEPARTURE

After Yr's birth, all of the female chimpanzees were put on birth control so they wouldn't have any new babies. The community was not to grow any larger; this was to be the fixed group, with Julius as its leader. His life had reached its final chapter, and now it would simply be a matter of the king shuffling around on the game board in a controlled manner, mediating conflicts and maintaining his position as the unopposed leader for as long as possible.

But in October of 2013, it was time for Bini to take leave of the community. While the other Kristiansand chimpanzees were crossbreeds of differing subspecies, a DNA test revealed that Bini was a purer subspecies of West African descent. The international breeding cooperative, of which the zoo was a member, requested that she be transferred to a Dutch zoo with a group made up of the same subspecies. She was thirty-nine years old but still able to bear young.

Bini was anesthetized and transported via car and ferry to the Netherlands. Her transfer was painful, both for the chimpanzees and for her keepers in Kristiansand, but the experience was more natural than one might imagine. In the wild, female chimpanzees often go back and forth between different communities—one of nature's own protections against incest and inbreeding. The fact that Bini was now leaving to join another colony and perhaps to mother babies with the new male chimpanzees there, was as it should be. Only slightly less natural was the fact that she rode in a car to get there.

Following Bini's departure and Linus's death, there were now nine chimpanzees left in the group: Julius, Dixi, Josefine, Miff, Jane, Tobias, Knerten, Julius Junior and Yr. Knerten, Tobias and Junior were theoretically almost old enough to unite and fight Julius for joint leadership of the group. Junior was the most frequent instigator; he loved a good brawl and was always ready for a fight but with Bini's departure, he had lost valuable motherly support. Power games within a chimpanzee community depend on alliances, and without a mother, Junior didn't stand a chance. Knerten and Tobias still had their mothers, but their mothers, Miff and Dixi, were often rivals. They scuffled for the alpha female position that had been left vacant by Bini. Their fights were also an indirect battle over who would get to be Julius's successor.[296] In May 2016, they got into a serious altercation. As the fight broke out on Chimp Island, the keepers had no way of intervening and both Julius and Junior got caught up in the brawl. The situation began to take a serious turn as the two females tussled with each other, and their fighting soon spun completely out of control. Julius tried desperately to separate the two females but ended up with a serious bite on his lip. When this happened, however, the fight quickly broke up. The impulse to let up when someone gets hurt is a strong one.

The bite on Julius's lip was so deep that he had to be put under anesthesia for stitches. Keeper Tanya Minchin had trained Julius to accept shots. She had taught him to put his arm through the bars so she could give him a shot of saline solution and then rewarded him each time he accepted the treatment. Now she was able to reap the benefits of her work, as Julius allowed her to give him a shot of anesthetic in his arm. Rolf Arne Ølberg stitched up the wound on his lip, did a thorough health examination, and since he now had the chance, pulled a tooth that had been bothering Julius for a long time. They painted purple nail polish on Julius's nails so that when he woke up, he would pay more attention to his glamorous nails than to picking at the wound.[297]

Julius roused out of anesthesia and returned to his group to resume leadership. However, on Tuesday, October 25, 2016, all hell broke loose again. A new fight developed in the sleeping quarters between Julius and Dixi or Miff, the keepers don't know for certain as no one saw them. It might have started as a fight between Dixi and Miff, in which Julius intervened and was wounded. He received a gash on his left leg, and once again, had to be put under and stitched up. This time, Carl Christian Glad, who by this point had grown up and become a dentist, came to check Julius's teeth. The zoo had employed Carl Christian for several of the zoo animals before, but this was his first time checking the teeth of his old friend.[298] The teeth were fine, Julius handled the anesthetic well the second time too, his injuries healed and he continued his leadership in the group. These fights demonstrated that he was still able to step in and break up conflicts when necessary.

In a wild community, Julius would have been too old now to keep his place on the throne. But in a captive community such as this, he may still be able to remain the alpha male for years to come. Ideally, his eventual demotion will happen gradually and gently. Some zoos have observed that alpha males move to a second-in-command position in their later years.

Julius might go on living in this way for several decades. Or he may have a heart attack like his father and die instantly. There is no plan for the future. Whatever happens, happens. But for the time being, Julius remains in power.

Chapter 12

THESE EYES

*"An animal's eyes have the power to speak a great
language. Independently, without needing co-operation
of sounds and gestures, most forcibly when they rely
wholly on their glance, the eyes express the mystery."* [299]

MARTIN BUBER

N THE COURSE of Julius's life, conditions for animals in the
Kristiansand Zoo have vastly improved. When the first
chimpanzees arrived at the park in 1976, the employees
knew little to nothing about keeping primates. They fumbled
about and did their best, running back and forth to tend all
of the different species in their collection. Today there is full-
time staff dedicated solely to the chimpanzees, and their primary task is to stimulate the chimpanzees both physically and
intellectually. Activities are varied, offering new challenges
and unfamiliar situations in order to engage and sharpen
the chimpanzees' minds. [300] The food has improved too. The

chimps are given less fruit and more vegetables, along with specially imported nuts containing all of the important nutrients they need to thrive. The chimpanzees in the group have grown fuller and healthier. Miff has lost her double chin, and Julius has shed about 44 pounds. The community's basic routines have also been modified. The keepers have stopped separating the chimpanzees in the evenings and putting them into individual sleeping quarters. Nowadays, they are allowed to sleep together in the open enclosure. They are given wool blankets and build "nests" for themselves, not unlike the way they might settle down for the night in the wild. This practice has helped them to be more harmonious.[301] While they previously had to spend entire winters indoors for fear that they might get sick from the cold Norwegian climate, their enclosure has now been upgraded to allow the chimpanzees to go outside any day of the year, except on those days when the moat has frozen over, as they would be able to simply saunter right out into the zoo. But otherwise they can now choose for themselves when and for how long they want to be outside in the winter. If they get cold and wet, they can simply come inside to the warmth of the jungle enclosure. In addition, a path has been created leading to the roof of the enclosure so that it is now possible for them to climb up and get fresh air whenever they want. Miff, in particular, is fond of climbing up to get some snow. None of the chimps has gotten sick from close contact with snow. On the contrary, health conditions among the group have never been better. The practice of medicating chimpanzees in order to maintain peace in the community, as was common in the 1980s, has today become unimaginable.

On the other hand, for wild chimpanzees living in Central Africa, developments over the same window of time have been catastrophic. Their population numbers are in a free fall. When Julius was born, there were approximately one million wild chimpanzees; the number remaining today may be under 200,000. If this rate of extermination continues undeterred, and if Julius lives the longest possible chimpanzee life, it is quite possible that he risks outliving the last of the world's wild chimpanzees. But it is not only chimpanzees that are at risk. Other animal species vanish daily from the earth. In Julius's lifetime alone, half of the world's animal populations have been lost. In other words, twice as many animals existed in the world when Julius was born as there currently are today. During his lifetime, half of the Arctic ice cap has melted due to human-caused global warming.[302] In between every birthday that Julius has celebrated, an area of rain forest the size of Denmark has vanished.

Over half of the world's species live in the rain forest. Life-forms that we scarcely recognize are also disappearing. When Jane Goodall went into the Tanzanian jungle in the summer of 1960, risking her life to study the everyday habits of wild chimpanzees, she opened the door to a new world. There is still so much we don't know or understand about wild chimpanzees. Since Goodall's initial work, researchers have discovered that chimpanzees have culture and that there are cultural variations to the methods used to solve practical tasks in different groups, independent of biological conditions. In some chimpanzee communities, for instance, sharp sticks are utilized during the hunt while other communities use only their hands. In West Africa, chimpanzees use stones to crack nuts; this has never been observed in East Africa.[303] And these cultural practices become traditions that are passed on from generation to generation. Very recently, a research group analyzing the variation between the Y-chromosomes of male chimpanzees from eight different chimpanzee communities was able to estimate the time span back to the oldest common ancestor and thereby draw conclusions about how old these different cultures might be. Among the eight communities studied, the cultures varied a few hundred years old to some that were over 2,000 years old.[304] This means that there are chimpanzee cultures residing deep in the rain forests whose long cultural traditions are several thousand years old. These communities may soon vanish forever.

Fewer and fewer of the people who work with chimpanzees in captivity are able to hold back from getting engaged in the larger fight to save wild chimpanzees. Jane Goodall has even mentioned a large research conference, which she attended in 1986, at which chimpanzee experts from around the world gathered to present documentation on wild chimpanzees being threatened by human development. Goodall said that she attended the conference as a chimpanzee researcher and returned home as a chimpanzee activist. She was forced to re-prioritize her career because she could not simply sit by and passively watch what was happening. Many of the Kristiansand zookeepers have likewise become engaged in rehabilitation projects for wild chimpanzees in the Congo. For many of zookeepers, it feels like something they must do, as though Julius and the other chimpanzees in the Ape Jungle require it of them. It is almost as though they are pleading with their mysterious eyes.

Anyone who has worked with chimpanzees can talk about the inscrutable chimpanzee gaze. In opposition to a gorilla, who will interpret direct eye contact as a challenge, a human may stare straight into a chimpanzee's eyes without upsetting them. If you do so, you will see something there. Their eyes radiate life or intelligence in a way that one does not see among other animals. It's a difficult experience to put into words. It is not unlike the feeling of recognizing someone's eyes through a mask. That feeling of something known and unknown at the same time.

Billy Glad's journal from Julius's first year is consistently written in plain medical-professional prose. He broke this style only once: the first time he described Julius's gaze, "I am sitting with you in my lap," Glad wrote, addressing Julius directly in an untypical manner: "You are lying looking up at me with your large, brown and clear eyes. You have such a serious face, little man—like an old man. You look so wise, so quizzical. And yet your gaze is so clear and open."[305] Frans de Waal, who has stared into many more pairs of chimpanzee eyes than most of us ever will, verifies the experience: "If we look directly and deeply into a chimpanzee's eyes, we will see an intelligent and self-confident personality staring back at us," he wrote.[306] Those human individuals who have been closest to Julius can still sit close up to his bars and share deep eye contact with him. When Ane Moseid visits, Julius always wants to play their old game where one of them places a stick or piece of straw in their mouth while they sit on either side of the bars. Then the other tries to grab the stick with their lips, as they used to do in her room in Vennesla in 1980, and she looks straight into his still, dark eyes.[307]

It is as though the chimpanzee gaze is making an appeal to us. We once captured exotic animals and put them in cages and stared at them in order to celebrate our victory over wild nature. Now they stand there staring back at us, fruitlessly trying to remind us of our duty to that same nature. Perhaps this is the mystery of the chimpanzee's eyes? That we seem to see a duty and responsibility in them, a responsibility for Julius's wild relatives and for all of the animal species and life forms that we are currently destroying. That we as humans have a duty to look after a future in which new miracles might go on multiplying in the African jungles, many hundreds of years after Julius has died and is forgotten. That new electrical impulses in the small, not-yet-developed heart chambers of unborn chimpanzees will still be able to send the same message that Julius's heart received once, in May of 1979: beat, tiny heart, beat!

NOTES

Chapter 1: Nature and Nurture

1   William Glad's Journal, author's collection, 02.12.1980. William Glad kept an accurate and detailed journal during the period when Julius lived among humans. This journal is the most valuable archival source for this chapter, and indeed throughout this work.

2   With regards to the rain: www.yr.no/sted/Norge/Oslo/Oslo/Oslo/ almanakk.html?dato=1979-05-17.

3   Interview with Åse Gunn Mosvold Hogga, 09.19.2016. The observation report cited by Skeie 1996: 27.

4   Interview with Åse Gunn Mosvold Hogga, 09.19.2016.

5   State Archives in Kristiansand, D/1360, Box 22, Folder: K. Myhre— correspondence with the Agricultural Department 1974–77, veterinary section of the Agricultural Department v/ Reidar Vollan to the Kristiansand Zoo v/ Knut Myhre, 01.13.1976.

6   Interview with Edvard Moseid, 10.21.2016, State Archives in Kristiansand, D/1360, Box 22, Folder: K. Myhre—correspondence with the Agricultural Department 1974–77, veterinary section of the Agricultural Department v/ Reidar Vollan to the Kristiansand Zoo v/ Knut Myhre, 01.13.1976 and Kristiansand Zoo v/ Knut Myhre to the Agricultural Department, Veterinary Director, 03.08.1977 and "The application for dispensation from the prohibition on importing animals and birds from abroad," Concept, u.d.

7   Interview with Åse Gunn Mosvold Hogga, 09.19.2016.

8   Goodall, 1986: 231 based on Wrangham and Smuts 1980. The exact numbers in this register is that they use 47 percent of their waking hours eating and 13 percent on moving around in search for food.

9   tv.nrk.no/serie/norge-rundt/DVNR03003911/30-09-2011#del=1&t=14m.

10 *Fædrelandsvennen*, 08.09.1980, William Glad's journal, 02.12.1980, author's collection, and interview with William and Reidun Glad, 02.01.2016.

11 de Waal 2007: 65.

12 Interview with Gunn Reinertsen, 09.29.2016 and Åse Gunn Mosvold Hogga, 09.19.2016.

13 William Glad's journal, 02.12.1980, author's collection.

14 Interview with William Glad, 02.01.2016.

15 Interview with Reidun Glad, 02.01.2016.

Chapter 2: Happy Days

16 de Waal 2007: 3.

17 William Glad's journal, 02.12.1980, author's collection.

18 William Glad's journal, 02.12.1980, author's collection, and interview with Reidun and William Glad, 02.01.2016.

19 Harari 2016: 332.

20 William Glad's journal, 02.13.1980, author's collection.

21 "Great apes communicate cooperatively," esciencenews.com, 05.24.2016.

22 Goodall 1986: 16 f., "A clear, molecular view of how human color vision evolved," esciencenews.com, 12.19.2014.

23 William Glad's journal, 02.12.1980, author's collection.

24 William Glad's journal, 02.27.1980, author's collection.

25 Interview with Marit Espejord, formerly Moseid, 04.27.2016, Ane Moseid-Vårhus, 01.29.2017 and Edvard Moseid, 10.21.2016.

26 de Waal 2016: 25.

27 Interview with Edvard Moseid, 10.21.2016.

28 Interview with William Glad, 02.01.2016, State Archives in Kristiansand, D/1360, Box 17, Folder: K. Myhre, diverse annual releases and reports regarding the status of the zoo 1976–78, "Report on conditions in the Kristiansand Zoo 1978."

29 de Waal 2007.

30 de Waal 2007.

31 de Waal 2007: 70.

32 de Waal 2007: 166 and 72 f.

33 State Archives in Kristiansand, D/1360, Box 33, Folder 3.0 1970–85, "Discussion on current primatological problems (with chimpanzees) and a report from the trip to Zurich, Basel and Arnhem from March 12–14, 1980."

34 William Glad's journal, 03.31.1980, author's collection.

35 Sveindal 2006: 176.

36 William Glad's journal, 04.14.1980, author's collection.

37 William Glad's journal, 04.16.1980, author's collection.

38 Interview with Marit Espejord, formerly Moseid, 04.27.2016, Ane Moseid-Vårhus, 01.29.2017, Edvard Moseid, 10.21.2016, the *Venneslaposten* newspaper, 06.08.1983, Sveindal 2006: 69 f.

39 Goodall 1986: 11.

40 Goodall 1986: 34, Temerlin 1975: 120. Washoe continued learning signs for the rest of her life. When she died in 2007, she had mastered around 350 signs. But her alleged combination of words such as "water" and "bird" to indicate "swan" are controversial and not universally accepted in the research community. Claims have been made that Washoe may have meant "there is water" and "there is bird" because she saw both objects. Documentation of this type of the use of combining signs would have required a controlled test regime in which both meaningful and meaningless combinations were registered. See de Waal 2016: 98–106 for a skeptical critique of the great ASL-wave in primate research.

41 Temerlin 1975: 49.

42 Diamond 2014: 251 f.

43 Savage-Rumbaugh and Lewin 1994: 40.

44   en.wikipedia.org/wiki/Lucy_(chimpanzee).

45   *Fædrelandsvennen*, 08.09.1980.

46   Interview with Marit Espejord, formerly Moseid, 04.27.2016, Klingsheim 2009, Skeie 1996: 47.

47   Interview with Åse Gunn Mosvold Hogga, 09.19.2016, Edvard Moseid 10.21.2016, Marit Espejord, formerly Moseid, 04.27.2016, Ane Moseid-Vårhus, 01.29.2017, William Glad's journal, 09.02.1980, author's collection, *Fædrelandsvennen*, 08.17.1980, Skeie 1996: 50 and Sveindal 2006: 85.

Chapter 3: A Room of One's Own

48   Köhler 1925: 282.

49   Goodall 2000.

50   Goodall 2000.

51   Goodall 1986: 581 f.

52   NRK, "The Chimpanzee Julius," episode 1:4, tv.nrk.no/serie/sjimpansen-julius/FSK000003280/01-12-1980.

53   Interview with Marit Espejord, formerly Moseid, 04.27.2016.

54   William Glad's journal, 10.3–10.5.1980, author's collection.

55   William Glad's journal, 09.20.1980, author's collection.

56   William Glad's journal, 10.25.1980, author's collection.

57   William Glad's journal, 11.06.1980, author's collection.

58   William Glad's journal, 11.17.1980, author's collection.

59   William Glad's journal, 1.19.1980, author's collection.

60   Interview with Edvard Moseid, 10.21.2016.

61   William Glad's journal, 12.09.1980, author's collection.

62   William Glad's journal, 1.216.1980, author's collection.

63   de Waal 2003: 67. But there are other animals, outside of the realm of mammals, who have the same degree of self-awareness and who perform just as well on this mirror test, among them several birds in the crow family. In addition, dolphins, orca whales and later also elephants have passed the test.

64   de Waal 2007: 128.

65   Goodall 1986, based on Gardner and Gardner 1969.

66   Goodall 1986: 36, according to Hayes and Hayes 1951.

Chapter 4: Home for Christmas

67   *Fædrelandsvennen*, 12.23.1981

68   Lystrup 2016: 50.

69   NRK, "The Chimpanzee Julius," episode 2:4, tv.nrk.no/serie/sjimpansen-julius/FSK000005381/15-02-1982.

70   NRK, "The Chimpanzee Julius," episode 2:4, tv.nrk.no/serie/sjimpansen-julius/FSK000005381/15-02-1982.

71   William Glad's journal, 03.08.1981, author's collection.

72   *VG*, 07.20.1981.

73   Interview with Edvard Moseid, 10.21.2016.

74   NRK, "The Chimpanzee Julius," episode 3:4,tv.nrk.no/serie/sjimpansen-julius/FSK000005481/22-02-1982.

75   Interview with Edvard Moseid, 10.21.2016.

76   *Fædrelandsvennen*, 08.03 and 08.04.1978, *Dagbladet Sørlandet*, 08.03.1978, *Nå*, 08.12.1978, The State Archives in Kristiansand, D/1360, Box 17 Folder: K. Myhre, diverse releases and reports regarding animal conditions from 1976–78, "Report on the conditions in Kristiansand Zoo 1978." Now 08.12.1978.

77   Klingsheim 2009.

78   Skeie 1996: 69.

79   The State Archives in Kristiansand, D/1360, Box 35, "Report on death / male chimpanzee 'Dennis,' age 13 Kristiansand Zoo."

80   Interview with Billy Glad, 02.01.2016, Edvard Moseid, 10.21.2016, Åse Gunn Mosvold Hogga, 09.19.2016.

81   "How chimps deal with death: Studies offer rare glimpses," esciencenews.com, 26.4.2010.

82   de Waal 2003: 56.

83   Interview with Edvard Moseid, 10.21.2016, Marit Espejord, formerly Moseid, 04.27.2016, Ane Moseid-Vårhus, 01.29.2017 and www.yr.no/ sted/Norge/Vest-Agder/Kristiansand/Kjevik_målestasjon/almanakk .html?dato=1981-12-24.

84   Interview with Billy Glad, 02.01.2016.

Chapter 5: Monkey Business

85   Yerkes 1925: 82.

86   Hancocks 2007: 95.

87   Rothfels 2002: 12, Goodall 1986: 6.

88   Rothfels 2002: 19, Hancocks 2007: 96.

89   Rothfels 2002.

90   Sveindal 2006: 12.

91   Flinterud 2012: 97.

92   Sveindal 2006: 46–49.

93   State Archives in Kristiansand, D/1360, Box 196, "Report on the conditions in Kristiansand Zoo in 1982," Gudbrand Hval, 04.05.1983.

94   Glad and Nesland 1986.

95   State Archives in Kristiansand, D/1360, Box 196, "Report on the chimpanzees (Pan troglodytes) 1983."

96   Goodall 1986: 415.

97   Goodall 1986: 75.

98   Interview with Åse Gunn Mosvold Hogga, 09.19.2016.

99   Fædrelandsvennen, 04.21.1982.

100 William Glad's journal, 05.18.–05.20.1982, author's collection.

101 Interview with Åse Gunn Mosvold Hogga, 09.19.2016.

102 VG, 04.23.1983.

103 VG, 05.10.1983.

104 Aftenposten, 07.27.1984.

105 *Aftenposten*, 08.02.1984.

106 *Aftenposten*, 08.03.1984.

107 *Aftenposten*, 03.12.1984, Sveindal 2006: 74, *Agderposten*, 01.10.2015, *Aftenposten*, 08.02.1992 and *Aftenposten*, 12.30.1992.

108 *VG*, 07.30.1983.

109 *VG*, 07.30.1983.

110 NRK, "The Chimpanzee Julius," episode 4:4, tv.nrk.no/serie/sjimpansen-julius/FSKO24000183/12-03-1984.

111 The most well-known examples are perhaps Franz Kafka's "A Report to an Academy"; the Danish author Peter Høeg's international best-seller *The Woman and the Ape*; and the world's very first modern detective story, Edgar Allan Poe's "The Murders in the Rue Morgue" from 1841, in which it turns out that an escaped orangutan is behind the horrendous double murder.

112 Lever 2009. *Me Cheeta: The Autobiography* is of course neither an autobiography nor an attempt to portray the development of this chimpanzee's life. Rather, it is a parody of genre of memoir by washed-up Hollywood stars written by James Lever and presented as the memoir of one of the greatest stars ever to live, Cheeta. Not only is the book a work of fiction, the character Cheeta is fictional as well. There was never only a single chimpanzee acting in all of these films but, in fact, several. There may even have been multiple chimpanzees acting in a single film, each of them being used to display their particular tricks or whatever type of skills they had mastered.

113 Hals Gylseth and Toverud 2001. Julia Pastrana's body resided in Oslo until February 2013. Thereafter it was handed over to the Mexican embassy in Norway, returned to Mexico and buried in a Catholic church-yard in Sinaloa de Leyva, close to where Pastrana had been born 179 years earlier.

Chapter 6: A Fugitive Crosses His Tracks

114 Goodall 1986: 170.

115 *Fædrelandsvennen*, 05.03.1984.

116 State Archives in Kristiansand, D/1360, Box 197, Folder: Working group for chimpanzees "Sketch of training enclosure for small chimpanzees," William R. Glad.

117 "Early maternal loss has lifelong effects on chimpanzees," esciencenews. com, 11.11.2015.

118 "Chimpanzees raised as pets or performers suffer long-term effects on their behavior," esciencenews.com, 09.24.2014.

119 State Archives in Kristiansand, D/1360, box 196, Autopsy Report, 10.02.1985: Veterinary Institute from Bjørn Lium to Dr. William Glad.

120 *Allers*, 19/1986.

121 State Archives in Kristiansand, D/1360, Folder: Working group for chimpanzees "Sketch of training enclosure for small chimpanzees," William R. Glad.

122 State Archives in Kristiansand, D/1360, Folder: Working group for chimpanzees, Minutes from the working group meeting on 10.29.1985.

123 State Archives in Kristiansand, D/1360, Folder: Working group for chimpanzees, Minutes from the working group meetings 1985, 1986.

124 *Aftenposten*, 07.12.1986.

125 *Fædrelandsvennen*, 02.27.1987.

126 *Fædrelandsvennen*, 02.27.1987.

127 de Waal 2007: x–xi, Köhler 1925.

128 Interview with Knut Uppstad 02.02.2017.

129 de Waal 2005: 138 and de Waal 2013: 152.

130 Interview with Åse Gunn Mosvold Hogga, 09.19.2016 and *VG*, 07.01.1987.

131 William Glad's journal, 06.05.1987, author's collection.

132 de Waal 2007: 79.

133 de Waal 2007: 105. Frans de Waal didn't believe there was any other option but to use the term *reconciliation* to describe this widespread and well-documented behavior, a term that was controversial at first in the research milieu due to its anthropomorphic connotations but which was gradually accepted when the behavior became so explicitly documented. Chimpanzee researchers—and most likely chimpanzee

biographers as well—are still often criticized for anthropomorphizing, in other words that the authors describe an animal's behavior in human terms, thereby making it more similar to ourselves than it is in reality. Frans de Waal warns against such criticism. He believes that the traditional research community has missed out on and failed to see valuable insights expressly due to their fear of being accused of anthropomorphizing. De Waal came up with the term *anthropodenial* for this instinctive reflex to dismiss all use of human terms even when studying a species that is as close to humans as the chimpanzee. De Waal believes the use of such human terms does much more to obscure and debilitate research if one is studying creatures that are vastly different from humans, for example applying labels such as "soldier," "queen" and "worker" to ants. But by refusing to speak about how chimpanzees greet or kiss one another or enter into longstanding friendships, that is, that they practice clearly documented behaviors and behavioral patterns which correspond to similar behaviors amongst humans, the effect is not a more objective science but rather misunderstood analyses. By insisting on referring to a chimpanzee kiss as "mouth-to-mouth contact" in order to avoid anthropomorphizing the chimpanzees, one fails to correctly understand the animal's behavior. De Waal believes that this is akin to relating the moon's gravitation to something other than the Earth's just because we view the Earth as something special (de Waal 2016: 22–28). According to de Waal, this fear of anthropomorphizing chimpanzees is remnant from a pre–Darwinian way of thinking, as though the gap between humans and the rest of nature is so vast that it is principally impossible to apply insights and words from the human life to our understanding of other animals.

134 de Waal 2007: 107.

135 *Norsk Ukeblad* nr. 25, 1987.

136 *Dagbladet*, 07.20.1987.

137 *Norsk Ukeblad* nr. 25, 1987.

138 *Norsk Ukeblad* nr. 25, 1987, *Hjemmet* nr. 25, 1987.

139 Diamond 2014: 80 f.

140 de Waal 2007: 152.

141 Goodall 1986: 483 f.

142 de Waal 2007: 172.

143 de Waal 2007: 154 f.

144 Diamond 2014: 84.

145 Goodall 1986: 448.

146 *Agderposten*, 10.22.2002, interview with Åse Gunn Mosvold Hogga, 09.19.2016, Edvard Moseid, 10.21.1016 and Marit Espejord, formerly Moseid, 04.27.2016.

147 *Aftenposten*, 08.01.1987.

148 *VG*, 07.30.1988, *Nordlys* 08.01.1988, *Allers*, 36/1988.

149 Interview with Åse Sundbø, 09.16.2016.

150 Interview with Edvard Moseid, 10.21.2016.

150 *Fædrelandsvennen*, 19.9.1988.

151 Sveindal 2006: 151 f. and 104, *Fædrelandsvennen*, 31.5.1991, *Bergens Tidende*, 07.03.1991, *VG*, 07.03.1991, *Dagbladet*, 07.03.1991.

152 Interview with Kristin Fausa Island, 10.11.2016.

153 *Fædrelandsvennen*, 05.25.1989, interview with Kristin Fausa Island, 10.11.2016 and NTB, here quoted from *Hamar Arbeiderblad*, 05.31.1989.

154 "Swimming like humans," Andreas R. Graven, forskning.no, 08.18.2003, 05:00.

155 *Aftenposten*, 04.19.1990.

Chapter 7: Crime and Punishment

156 *VG*, 07.07.1992.

157 *Aftenposten*, 01.06.1990.

158 *VG*, 26.6.1991, *Se og Hør* nr. 33, 1990.

159 *Aftenposten*, 04.23.1991.

160 *VG*, 05.23.1991.

161 *Fædrelandsvennen*, 05.23.1991.

162 *Fædrelandsvennen*, 05.23.1991.

163 NRK *Kveldsnytt*, 05.22.1991, *Fædrelandsvennen*, 05.23.1991, *Agderposten*, 05.23.1991 and *Dagbladet*, 05.23.1991.

164 NRK *Dagsrevyen*, 05.23.1991.

165 Interview with Gunn Holen Robstad, 10.14.2016.

166 NTB, 06.25.1991, *Fædrelandsvennen*, 06.25.1991, *Aftenposten* 06.26.1991, *Bergens Tidende*, 06.26.1991, *Adresseavisen*, 06.26.1991, VG, 06.26.1991.

167 VG, 06.26.1991.

168 Interview with Åse Sundbø, 09.16.2016, *Fædrelandsvennen*, 09.10.1991.

169 Interview with Oddvar Ivarson, 02.05.2017.

170 Interview with Oddvar Ivarson, 02.05.2017.

171 *Dagbladet*, 10.08.2009.

172 de Waal 2013: 187. The Arnhem group has to go inside every night, and none of the chimpanzees are fed until they are all in. On one evening when the weather was particularly beautiful, two female chimpanzees refused to go inside and thus delayed the feeding for the rest of the group by several hours. When they finally came inside, they were put into their separated sleeping pens like all the other group members. The following day, however, when they had all been released outside again, the entire group chased and punished the two females physically for breaking the rules the day before. The group taught both of them to obey this rule, although the rule was a human construct. On that evening, the two females were the first to run inside when the entrance doors were opened.

173 de Waal 2013: 128. Moreover, a rule often becomes most visible upon being broken. Breaking the rules of reciprocity is strictly sanctioned. In the Arnhem group, researchers once observed that a chimpanzee cheated by not acting on expected reciprocity. The female chimpanzee Puist had assisted the male Luit in a conflict with another male, Nikkie. Just afterwards, Nikkie wanted to take revenge on Puist, so she clearly requested assistance from Luit, to no avail. As soon as Nikkie was done with her, Puist charged Luit in a rage. She screamed in his face and chased him around the enclosure. For more on this, see de Waal 2003: 97.

174 de Waal 2003: 60.

175 Temerlin 1975, 164 f.

176 de Waal 2013: 46 f.

177 de Waal 2005: 151.

178 Interview with Gunn Reinertsen, 09.29.2016.

179 Temerlin 1975: 122.

180 Donovan and Anderson 2006: 190.

181 *VG*, 06.10.1992, NRK, 06.10.1992.

182 *VG*, 06.12.1992.

183 *VG*, 07.07.1992.

184 Interview with Oddvar Ivarson, 02.05.2017.

Chapter 8: Four Weddings and a Funeral

185 *Fædrelandsvennen*, 07.23.1996.

186 Interview with Åse Sundbø, 09.16.2016.

187 *Dagbladet*, 5.6.1993, *VG*, 06.05.1993.

188 *VG*, 06.21.1993.

189 Bråten 1998: 239.

190 *Aftenposten*, 06.25.1994 and 07.02.1994.

191 Flinterud 2012: 210 f.

192 *Agderposten*, 06.25.1994.

193 *Fædrelandsvennen*, 02.24.1994.

194 Lystrup 2016: 129.

195 Skeie 1996: 92.

196 Interview with Gunn Holen Robstad, 10.14.2016.

197 Interview with Åse Sundbø, 09.16.2016.

198 State Archives in Kristiansand, D/1360, Box 10, Animal Populations per 12.31.1995.

199 Interview with Arne Magne Robstad, 10.14.2016.

200 *Agderposten*, 03.06.1996 and 05.06.1996, *Fædrelandsvennen*, 03.06.1996.

201 *Fædrelandsvennen*, 04.16.1996.

202 *Fædrelandsvennen*, 04.24.1996, *VG*, 04.25.1996.

203 *VG*, 04.25.1996.

204 *Berlingske Tidende*, 04.24.1996.

205 *Berlingske Tidende*, 04.24.1996, *Klassekampen*, 05.07.1996.

206 *Dagbladet*, 05.06.1996.

207 NTB, 05.05.1996.

208 *VG*, 05.06.1996.

209 *Agderposten*, 05.11.1996, *VG*, 05.07.1996.

210 *Agderposten*, 05.25.1996.

211 *VG*, 05.31.1996.

212 Skeie 1996: 96.

213 *Fædrelandsvennen*, 06.01.1996, *Agderposten*, 06.01.1996.

214 *Dagbladet*, 06.01.1996.

215 *Agderposten*, 06.01.1996.

216 Interview with Edvard Moseid, 10.21.2016.

217 NTB, 05.31.1996.

218 *VG*, 06.01.1996.

219 *VG*, 06.01.1996.

220 de Waal 2007: 160, Goodall 1986: 470. Sometimes male chimpanzees succeed in pairing up with a rutting female for several days. Of the 258 short-term "monogamous" relationships that were observed in Gombe between 1966–83, the males were old enough to potentially have been the fathers of their sexual partners in only 18 percent of the cases.

221 *VG*, 06.02.1996.

222 *Agderposten*, 06.05.1996, *Vårt Land*, 01.03.1997.

223 *Agderposten*, 07.13.1996.

224 Interview with Arne Magne Robstad, 10.14.2016.

225 Diamond 2014: 304.

226 Eia and Ihle 2010.

227 *Dagbladet*, 07.14.1996.

228 *Dagbladet*, 07.19.1996.

229 *Fædrelandsvennen*, 07.23.1996.

230 *Fædrelandsvennen*, 12.27.1997, *Agderposten*, 12.27.1997 and interview with Arne Magne Robstad, 10.14.2016.

231 *Agderposten*, 01.02.1998.

232 *Agderposten*, 01.02.1998.

233 *Fædrelandsvennen*, 01.02.1998.

Chapter 9: The Child

234 de Waal 2007: 158.

235 *Aftenposten*, 10.11.1999. "Some cysts on her pelvic area have changed Julius's ex-wife into a tyrant. In believing herself to be a male, she has dethroned Julius," NRK observed on the same day.

236 news.mongabay.com/2016/10/jane-goodall-on-zoos-and-tech-as-conservation-tools/.

237 Interview with Edvard Moseid, 10.21.2016.

238 *Sunnmørsposten*, 08.22.2001.

239 *Agderposten*, 12.27.2000.

240 *Fædrelandsvennen*, 04.18.2002, *P4*, 04.18.2002, *Agderposten* 04.19.2002.

241 Interview with Arne Magne Robstad, 10.14.2016.

242 de Waal 2005: 43–47.

243 Interview with Arne Magne Robstad, 10.14.2016, Gunn Holen Robstad, 10.14.2016, Åse Sundbø, 09.16.2016 and William Glad, 02.01.2016.

244 *Agderposten*, 06.04.2003, NRK district 06.04.2003, NTB, 06.04.2003 *P4*, 06.04.2003, *Stavanger Aftenblad*, 06.04.2003, *VG*, 06.04.2003.

245 *VG*, 12.29.2002.

246 Interview with Åse Sundbø, 09.16.2016.

247 *Dagbladet*, 04.07.2004.

248 *Dagbladet*, 04.13.2004, *Dagsavisen*, 10.14.2005.

249 Goodall 1986: 25.

250 YouTube is brimming with videos of elephants painting pictures of themselves holding a paintbrush in their trunks. But these impressive self-portraits are most often a commercial trick. There is no reason to believe that the elephants visualize their art or see the basic similarities between their drawings and themselves; the elephants are rather performing learned behaviors taught to them by their keepers.

251 Diamond 2014: 189 ff.

252 Diamond 2014: 186.

253 *P4*, 05.03.2004.

254 *P4*, 05.03.2004.

255 de Waal 2003: 140 f.

256 *P4*, 08.27.2004.

Chapter 10: King of the Apes

257 Shakespeare 1988: *King Henry IV, Part II*, act III, scene i.

258 Interview with Rune Landås, 10.20.2016.

259 Harari 2016: 35.

260 Interview with Rune Landås, 10.20.2016.

261 The film *Julius tilbake til flokken* (Julius back in the group), Svein Tallaksen and Kalle Fürst, Mediaservice 2006, Accessible on Zoo TV. And interview with Rune Landås, 10.20.2016.

262 *Julius tilbake til flokken* (Julius back in the group), Svein Tallaksen and Kalle Fürst, Mediaservice 2006, Accessible on Zoo TV. And interview with Rune Landås, 10.20.2016.

263 *Julius tilbake til flokken* (Julius back in the group), Svein Tallaksen and Kalle Fürst, Mediaservice2006, accessible on Zoo TV. And interview with Rune Landås, 10.20.2016.

264 *Dagbladet*, 12.23.2005.

265 de Waal 2007: 158. During several years of study in Gombe in Tanzania, only a single male exception to this rule was ever observed. The male

chimpanzee Goblin was always aggressive toward young chimps that interrupted him during sex and ended up with a phobia of sorts in which he could no longer initiate mating if young chimpanzees were nearby. (Goodall 1986: 368).

266 *Agderposten*, 11.11.2006.

267 *VG*, 02.05.2007.

268 de Waal 2003: 124.

269 "Sex differences in chimpanzees' use of sticks as play objects resemble those of children," Richard W. Wrangham and Sonya M. Kahlenberg, *Current Biology*, 12.21.2010. Discussed in "A stick for a doll," Bjørnar Kjensli, research no. 12.22.2010 (Norwegian source).

270 de Waal 2013: 80. Based on the work of James Rilling's research team.

271 de Waal 2005: 109. Another evolutionary strategy to shield the environment of one's young is the human system of falling in love and monogamy. In this case, the father may feel relatively safe that the children who are born are genetically his own and therefore must be protected rather than killed.

272 Interview with Rune Landås, 10.20.2016.

273 Tillberg 1990, Tillberg 2017 and www.youtube.com/watch?v=Rnb QMc9Zoue.

274 *Aftenposten*, 11.10.2007.

275 *VG*, 12.10.2007.

276 *VG*, 10.13–16.2007. In February 2017, Louise Tillberg published a book about Ola's fate, but she did not succeed in confirming whether or not Ola was still alive. After sending many messages to the zoo in Thailand, she finally received the somewhat confusing reply: "[e]ver since Ola has been at our park, she [*sic!*] has received the best care" (Tillberg 2017: 186).

277 *Agderposten*, 10.12.2007.

278 Interview with Marit Espejord, formerly Moseid, 04.27.2016.

279 Singer 2002.

280 Goodall 1974: 506 f.

281 Goodall 1986: 508 f.

282 Goodall 1986: 78.

283 Goodall 1986: 351 f.

Chapter 11: End Game

284 de Waal 2007: 30.

285 *Fædrelandsvennen*, 10.07.2009, NRK, 10.07.2009.

286 Hancocks 2007: 102.

287 NTB, 10.08.2009.

288 Interview with Ane Moseid-Vårhus, 01.29.2017.

289 Many controlled experiments have researched chimpanzees' memories. The Japanese researcher Tetsuro Matsuzawa taught the young chimpanzee Ayumu the numbers from one to nine. The numbers were arbitrarily positioned on a computer screen for a few seconds before disappearing and being replaced with blank squares. Ayumu was supposed to count from one to nine based on his memory of where the numbers had been located. Ayumu performed better than humans in this test, astonishing the researchers by his ability to achieve the activity just as easily even when the numbers were flashed and disappeared more and more quickly onto the screen. He only needed 210 milliseconds, or a fifth of a second, to memorize all of the numbers (de Waal 2016: 119–128). Other experiments have shown that chimpanzees can remember things they learned many years prior, even if they have not used their skill in the interim. In a Danish experiment, chimpanzees were offered a treat outside their cage out of reach of their hands. But after some pondering and trial and error, they figured out that they could reach the treat by using a rod to which they had access. Three years later, the experiment was repeated and all of the chimpanzees immediately went to get the rod to fetch the treats, indicating that they remembered what they had learned three years earlier even though they had not used or been reminded of this skill a single time since. (For more on this last point, see "Chimpanzees and orangutans remember the distant past events," esciencenews.com, 07.18.2013).

290 de Waal 2005: 235, de Waal 2007: 34 f.

291 Interview with Rune Landås, 10.20.2016, *Agderposten*, 09.09.2011.

292 Interview with Rune Landås, 10.20.2016.

293 Interview with Rune Landås, 10.20.2016 and TV2 Sumo, *The Zookeepers*, season 4, episode 1.

294 TV2 Sumo, *The Zookeepers*, season 4, episode 1, NTB, 05.07.2012.

295 As told in de Waal 2013: 207, based on the research of Tetsuro Matsuzawa.

296 Interview with Tanya Minchin, 12.02.2016.

297 Interview with Tanya Minchin, 12.02.2016 and www.fvn.no/nyheter/lokalt/Julius-36-matte-opereres-443666b.html.

298 *Fædrelandsvennen*, 11.03.2016.

Chapter 12: These Eyes

299 Buber 1937.

300 This has been researched among the Kristiansand chimpanzees as well. Per Holth, a professor at the Institute for Behavioral Sciences at the Oslo Metropolitan University, conducted an experiment in which two jùice machines were installed in Julius's sleeping quarters. When the machines were turned on, the chimpanzees were able to pull a lever to help themselves to juice or smoothies. It took a bit of time for the chimpanzees to understand the system. Holth was able to monitor and control the machines from his office in Oslo, and for the first period, he helped them to figure it out by releasing juice whenever they got close to the lever. As soon as they all understood the system, the experiment became gradually more advanced. Eventually, the chimpanzees had to pull on the levers of both machines at the same time to release the juice, and then the machines were placed further apart, requiring the cooperation of two individual chimpanzees in order to release the drink. As a signal to the chimpanzees that the machines had been turned on and that they were welcome to help themselves, the Julius song by Terje Formoe was played over the loud speakers. Julius still loved this song, he truly understood who it was about, he knew his own name and has always had a weakness for attention. It is the chimpanzees' ability to work together in organized cooperation for the good of the group that most captivates Holth, and perhaps this cooperation is even the basic prerequisite for culture. Holth has previously conducted similar

experiments with rats, which were in fact faster at cracking the code and figuring out how to get water themselves. In Kristiansand, Bini was the quickest one to figure out the system, while Julius required a surprisingly long time. In reality, it was Knerten who taught Julius how the machine worked, not unlike the way that young people can teach older adults to handle new technology. In the first days, Julius would sit lapping up the juice while Knerten worked the levers for him. But Julius eventually understood the system, even the new, more advanced version in which two chimpanzees had to work together to release the juice. He would often work together with Miff or Dixi, depending on his preference. Julius was as clear a leader regarding the juice machines as he was otherwise in the enclosure. He made strict decision about who would be allowed to enter his room, who was allowed to help themselves to juice, and who should get lost. Junior, who was the best and fastest at handling the levers, was barely allowed to enter the room. While Josefine and Tobias—the two chimpanzees who were released inside last when the colony had been reorganized with Julius as the alpha male—were the only two who seemed utterly uninterested.

301 Interview with Helene Axelsen and Hildegunn Johannesen, 01.13.2016.

302 Kolbert 2015: 141.

303 de Waal 2016: 80.

304 Langergraber et al. 2014.

305 William Glad's journal, 03.06.1980, author's collection.

306 de Waal 2007: 3

307 Interview with Ane Moseid-Vårhus, 01.29.2017.

BIBLIOGRAPHY

Bråten 1998: *Kommunikasjon og samspill. Fra fødsel til alderdom* (tr. Communication and interaction. From birth to old age), Stein Bråten, Tano Aschehoug, 1998

Børresen 1996: *Den ensomme apen. Instinkt på avveie*, (tr. The lonely ape. Misguided instinct) Bergljot Børresen. Gyldendal, 1996

Buber 1937: *I and Thou*, Martin Buber. Tr. by Ronald Gregor Smith. Edinburgh: T. & T. Clarke, 1937

Dawkins 1976: *The Selfish Gene*, Richard Dawkins, Oxford: First American Edition, 1976

de Waal 2003: *Good Natured: The Origins of Right and Wrong in Humans and Other Animals*, Frans de Waal, Harvard University Press, 2003

de Waal 2005: *Our Inner Ape*, Frans de Waal, Riverhead Books, 2005

de Waal 2007: *Chimpanzee Politics: Power and Sex among Apes. 25th Anniversary Edition*, Frans de Waal, The John Hopkins University Press, 2007

de Waal 2013: *The Bonobo and the Atheist: In Search of Humanism among the Primates*, Frans de Waal, W.W. Norton & Company, 2013

de Waal 2016: *Are We Smart Enough to Know How Smart Animals Are?*, Frans de Waal, W. W. Norton & Company, 2016

Diamond 2014: *The Third Chimpanzee: The Evolution and Future of the Human Animal*, Jared Diamond, Harper Perennial, 2006

Donovan and Anderson 2006: *Anthropology & Law*, James Donovan and Edwin Anderson, Berghahn Books, 2006

Eia and Ihle 2010: *Født sånn eller blitt sånn? Utro kvinner, sjalu menn og hvorfor oppdragelse ikke virker* (tr. Nature or nurture? Unfaithful women, jealous men and why a good upbringing doesn't work), Harald Eia and Ole-Martin Ihle, Gyldendal, 2010

Flinterud 2012: *A Polyphonic Bear: Animal and Celebrity in Twenty-First Century Popular Culture*, Guro Flinterud, The University of Oslo, Humanities Department, 2012

Gardner and Gardner 1969: "Teaching sign language to a chimpanzee," R.A. Gardner and B.T. Gardner, in *Science* 165: 664–672, 1969

Glad and Nesland 1986: "Focal Epithelial Hyperplasia of the Oral Mucosa in Two Chimpanzees (*Pan troglodytes*)," William R. Glad and Jahn M. Nesland, in *American Journal of Primatology* 10: 83–89, 1986

Goodall 1971: *In the Shadow of Man*, Jane van Lawick-Goodall, Houghton Mifflin Harcourt, 1971

Goodall 1986: *The Chimpanzees of Gombe: Patterns of Behavior*, Jane Goodall, The Belknap Press of Harvard University Press, 1986

Goodall 2000: *Reason for Hope: An Extraordinary Life*, Jane Goodall and Phillip Berman, Thorsons, 2000

Hals Gylseth and Toverud 2001: *Julia Pastrana. Apekvinnen*, (tr. Julia Pastrana. The ape woman) Christopher Hals Gylseth and Lars O. Toverud, Forlaget Press, 2001

Hancocks 2007: "Zoo Animals as Entertainment Exhibition," pp. 95–118 in *A Cultural History of Animals in the Modern Age*, Randy Malamud (ed.), Berg, 2007

Harari 2014: *Sapiens: A Brief History of Humankind*, Yuval Noah Harari, Vintage, 2014

Hayes 1951: *The Ape in Our House*, Cathy Hayes, Harper and Brothers, 1951

Hayes and Hayes 1951: "The intellectual development of a home-raised chimpanzee," Keith Hayes and Catherine Hayes, *Proceedings of the American Philosophical Society* 95: 105–109, 1951

Hessen 2007: *Natur. Hva skal vi med den?* (tr. Nature. What do we want from it?), Dag O. Hessen, Gyldendal, 2007

Hessen 2013: "Hvor unikt er mennesket?" (tr. How unique is the human?), Dag O. Hessen, pp. 57–77 in *Hvem er villest i landet her? Råskap mot dyr og natur I antropocen, menneskets tidsalder* (tr. Who is wildest in the land? Savagery toward animals and nature in anthropology, the age of humankind), Ragnhild Sollund, Morten Tønnessen and Guri Larsen (eds.), Scandinavian Academic Press, 2013

Hylland Eriksen and Hessen 1999: *Egoisme* (tr. Egotism), Thomas Hylland Eriksen and Dag O. Hessen, Aschehoug, 1999

Jonas 1993: *Das Prinzip Verantwortung. Versuch einer Ethik für die technologische Zivilisation*, (tr. The principal of responsibility. An ethical attempt for the technological civilization), Hans Jonas, Suhrkamp Verlag, 1993

Klingsheim 2009: *Julius*, Trygve Bj. Klingsheim, Cappelen Damm, 2009

Köhler 1948: *The Mentality of Apes*, Wolfgang Köhler, Routledge & Kegan Paul, 1948

Kolbert 2014: *The Sixth Extinction: An Unnatural History*, Elisabeth Kolbert, Henry Holt, 2014

Langergraber et al. 2014: "How old are chimpanzee communities? Time to the most recent common ancestor of the Y-chromosome in highly patrilocal societies," Kevin E. Langergraber, Carolyn Rowney, Grit Schubert, Cathy Crockford, Catherine Hobaiter, Roman Wittig, Richard W. Wrangham, Klaus Zuberbühler and Linda Vigilant, *Journal of Human Evolution* 69: 1–7, 2014

Lever 2009: *Me Cheeta: An Autobiography*, James Lever, Fourth Estate, 2009

Lindahl and Kuhn 2016: *Julius—et apeliv* (tr. Julius—a primate life), Lena Lindahl and Camilla Kuhn, self published, 2016

Lystrup 2016: *Dyrehviskeren* (tr. The animal whisperer). *Edvard Moseid og Dyreparken*, Marianne Lystrup, Portal Forlag, 2016

Malamud 2007: "Famous Animals in Modern Culture," Randy Malamud, pp. 1–26 in *A Cultural History of Animals in the Modern Age*, Randy Malmud (ed.), Berg, 2007

Marks 2002: *What It Means to Be 98% Chimpanzee: Apes, People, and Their Genes*, Jonathan Marks, University of California Press, 2002

Mjåland 2003: *Tiger i Parken* (tr. Tiger in the Park), Anne Enger Mjåland, Gyldendal, 2003

Oakley 1949: *Man the Tool-Maker*, Kenneth Oakley, Natural History Museum Publications, 1949

Rothfels 2002: *Savages and Beasts: The Birth of the Modern Zoo*, Nigel Rothfels, The John Hopkins University Press, 2002

Savage-Rumbaugh and Lewin 1994: *Kanzi: The Ape at the Brink of the Human Mind*, Sue Savage-Rumbaugh and Roger Lewin, John Wiley & Sons, 1994

Shakespeare 1988: *King Henry IV, Part II*, William Shakespeare, Bantam Classic, 1988

Short 1979: "Sexual selection and its component parts, somatic and genital selection, as illustrated by man and great apes," *Advances in the Study of Behavior*, 9: 131–158, 1979

Singer 1975: *Animal Liberation*, Peter Singer, HarperCollins, 1975

Skeie 1996: *Julius. En omvendt jungelbok* (tr. Julius. A reverse jungle book), Eyvind Skeie, Orion, 1996

Sveindal 2006: *40 dyrebare år. Historien om Dyreparken* (tr. 40 previous years. A history about the Kristiansand Zoo), Hans Martin Sveindal, Kristiansand Zoo ASA, 2006

Sveindal and Amtrup 2016: *Den levende parken. Dyreparken gjennom 50 år* (tr. The living park. 50 years of the Kristiansand Zoo), Hans Martin Sveindal and Jon Amtrup, self published, 2016

Temerlin 1975: *Lucy: Growing Up Human: A Chimpanzee Daughter in a Psychotherapist's Family*, Maurice K. Temerlin, Science and Behavior Books, 1975

Tillberg 1990: *Ola! Schimpansen Ola Norman* (tr. Ola! The chimpanzee Ola Norman), Louise Tillberg, Fischer & Co, 1990

Tillberg 2017: *Schimpansen Ola! Vem bryr sig om en apa?* (tr. The chimpanzee Ola! Who will take care of an ape?), Louise Tillberg, Gidlunds Förlag, 2017

Wise 2001: *Rattling the Cage: Toward Legal Rights for Animals*, Steven M. Wise, Da Capo Press, 2001

Woolf 1933: *Flush: A Biography*, Virginia Woolf, Hogarth Press, 1933

Wrangham and Smuts 1980: "Sex differences in behavioural ecology of chimpanzees in Gombe National Park, Tanzania," R.W. Wrangham and B. Smuts, in *Journal of Reproduction and Fertility*, 28: 13–31, 1980

Yerkes 1925: *Almost Human*, Robert M. Yerkes, The Century & Co, 1925

Zapffe 1996: *Om det tragiske* (tr. On the tragic), Peter Wessel Zapffe, Pax Forlag, 1996

INDEX

Page numbers followed by "n" and a number refer to an endnote; "plate" followed by a number refers to the pages of the photo insert.

ABOUT
THE AUTHOR

Norwegian author Alfred Fidjestøl has published several critically acclaimed biographies and history books about humans and cultural institutions. In 2014, Fidjestøl became the first non-fiction author ever to receive Gyldendal's Hunger Award. He was awarded the Norwegian Language (Språkprisen) Prize in 2017. *Almost Human* is his first chimpanzee biography.